SIXTY SQUADRON R.A.F. 1916 - 1919

VINTAGE AVIATION LIBRARY

Sixty Squadron, R.A.F. by Grp.-Capt. A.J.L. Scott

Recollections of an Airman by Lieut.-Col. L.A. Strange

King of Air Fighters by Flt.-Lieut. Ira Jones

Wings of War: A German Airman's Diary of the Last Year of the Great War by Rudolph Stark

A Flying Fighter: An American Above the Lines in France by Lieut. E.M. Roberts

The Flying Flea: How to Build and Fly It by Henri Mignet

French Warbirds by 'Vigilant' (Claud W. Sykes)

Flying Fury: Five Years in the Royal Flying Corps by James McCudden, VC

Over the Balkans and South Russia, 1917 - 1919 by H.A. Jones, M.C.

An Airman's Outings with the RFC by Alan Bott

etc., etc.

SIXTY SQUADRON R.A.F.

A HISTORY OF THE SQUADRON
1916 - 1919

by
GROUP-CAPTAIN A. J. L. SCOTT
C.B., M.C., A.F.C.

with a preface
by
THE RT. HON. LORD HUGH CECIL, M.P.

with additional material for this edition
by
SQN. LDR. D.W. WARNE
MRAeS, R.A.F. (Ret'd)

Greenhill Books, London
Presidio Press, California

This edition of *Sixty Squadron, R.A.F.* first published in 1990 by
Greenhill Books, Lionel Leventhal Limited, Park House,
1 Russell Gardens, London NW11 9NN
and
Presidio Press,
31 Pamaron Way, Novato, Ca.94947, U.S.A.

British Library Cataloguing in Publication Data
Scott, A. J. L.
Sixty Squadron, R.A.F: A History of the Squadron from its
formation. (Vintage Aviation Library No. 23).
1. Great Britain, Royal Air Force. Squadrons, history.
I. Title   II. Series   358.4'131'0941

ISBN 1-85367-049-9 Hardcover
ISBN 1-85367-050-2 Paperback

Publishing History
Sixty Squadron, R.A.F. was first published in 1920 (William Heinemann).
This edition reproduces the text and photographs
from the original edition, with additional photographs,
a new Introduction and two additional appendices.

Cover photographs of Nieuport 17 by kind courtesy of J. M. Bruce.

Greenhill Books
welcome readers' suggestions for books that might be added to
this series. Please write to us if there are titles which you would
like to recommend.

Printed by Antony Rowe Limited,
Chippenham, Wiltshire.

DEDICATED

TO THOSE WHO WERE

KILLED WITH THE SQUADRON

" Clean, simple, valiant, well beloved,
Flawless in faith and fame."

KIPLING

INTRODUCTION

Jack Scott: A Brief Appraisal

Alan John Lance Scott, known as 'Jack' and the author/
compiler of *Sixty Squadron, R.A.F. A History of the Squadron,
1916–1919*, was born on 29 June 1883; he was educated in
Sussex and then at Merton College, Oxford, where he
became Master of the University Draghounds. His resolute and fearless hunting ability was subsequently
reflected in his fighting career in the Royal Flying Corps.
He was fluent in German and was in Chambers with
F. E. Smith, later Lord Birkenhead, who as Lord
Chancellor was to write Scott's obituary for *The Times*.

When war broke out in August 1914, Jack Scott was a
junior officer in the Sussex Yeomanry; having gained his
RAeC Certificate (No. 975) he was then seconded to the
Royal Flying Corps, although he was well over the
average age for pilots at that time. His flying ability was
fundamentally poor, though this cannot be considered
abnormal for that period. Pilot training was grossly
inadequate until the Smith-Barry system was set up at
Gosport in 1917.

In 1915, when a pupil at the Central Flying School,
Scott was in a Henri Farman that broke up at 2,000 feet.
In the resulting crash he suffered two broken legs and
spent several months in hospital. After his release he
needed two sticks to enable him to walk and was given
some staff jobs.

Despite being refused permission to join a fighting squadron in France, he still managed to get there as a captain with 43 Squadron. Here he demonstrated his determination to get to grips with the enemy, albeit he needed help to get into the cockpit.

He was posted to command 60 Squadron, arriving on 10 March 1917. Air Commodore 'Grid' Caldwell summarises his short period in the post:

After Major Graves was lost, the replacement, Major Jack Scott, was a splendid choice and he continued to give 60 the leadership it had enjoyed under Graves. During Scott's reign, I believe the squadron could not have been in better fettle. We had leadership in the air (as CO he shot down a number of Huns, although only an indifferent pilot) as well as on the ground. He soon sized up the capabilities of his pilots, but I think his one fault was that being such a gentlemanly sort of chap, he thought the best of everybody and may have been a little tolerant in accepting combat claims from almost everyone when perhaps there was some doubt. There were claims from solo flights by individuals who had not proved themselves in patrol engagements, but Jack Scott saw the best in everyone.

His last sentence reflects similar comments by Scott's contemporaries when the German records were examined in detail in the mid-1920s, and little confirmatory evidence has come to light subsequently. Thus do self-generated legends occur!

By the time Scott reached 60 Squadron, regulations had confined squadron commanders to test and recreational flying. On 7 July, Major Scott returned from leave to find he had been posted to command a wing in a few weeks' time. However, shortly after 20.00 hours on the 10th, the klaxon sounded at Filescamp Farm and several Nieuports took off to intercept twelve enemy aircraft which were attacking troops near Monchy-le-Preux. Major Scott hobbled after them and joined up in time to engage nineteen enemy aircraft some twenty minutes later, just as they were turning towards their base. The enemy aircraft were green-painted Albatros scouts. It was the first time this colour scheme had been seen on the Arras Front. Scott and Billy Bishop made claims on this occasion, but Scott was wounded in the arm and taken to hospital.

OC 13th Wing ordered Major Scott to take command of 11th Wing immediately he came out of hospital, and after spending a week convalescing at Filescamp Farm, Scott moved on to command the 11th Wing on 23 July, 1917, now with the rank of lieutenant-colonel. Notification of the award of the MC for his service with 60 Squadron came shortly afterwards.

Within a few weeks, 60 Squadron, having moved to the Ypres sector, once more came under his command. By then it was equipped with SE5/SE5a fighters. In November 1917 Scott was posted as Commandant to the Central Flying School. A year later he was back in France as OC 13th Wing, where he had another crash though the consequent operations resulted in reduced lameness. However he was promptly posted back to Home Establishment to take command of No. 2 School of Aerial Navigation and Bomb Dropping at Andover. The award of the AFC followed.

After the war, Colonel (with effect from 22 May, 1919) Scott, now CB, MC, AFC, became Air Secretary to the Rt Hon Winston Churchill, Secretary of State for the War Office and the Air Force (to whom he gave flying instruction) and to his successor, Captain Rt Hon F. E. Guest. On 1 March, 1920, Scott was given the rank of group captain in the RAF, and was considered to be a future Chief of Air Staff. It was at this time he began the compilation of the history of 60 Squadron (PRO reference file AIR 1/693/21/20/60) that is here reprinted.

The brilliant career prospects for Jack Scott terminated on his death on 16th January 1922. After a skiing holiday at St. Moritz he succumbed to double pneumonia after a short illness, leaving a widow.

D. W. Warne
1990

PREFACE

THIS book tells the story of Squadron No. 60 of the Royal Flying Corps, afterwards of the Royal Air Force.

When the war began, in August 1914, the Royal Flying Corps was a very small body which sent four squadrons on active service and had a rudimentary training organisation at home. In those days the only functions contemplated for an airman were reconnaissance and occasionally bombing. Fighting in the air was almost unknown. The aeroplanes were just flying machines of different types, but intended to perform substantially the same functions. Gradually as the war continued specialisation developed. Fighting in the air began, machine guns being mounted for the purpose in the aeroplanes. Then some aeroplanes were designed particularly for reconnaissance, some particularly for fighting, some for bombing, and so on. It was in the early part of this period of specialisation that Squadron No. 60 was embodied. And, as this narrative tells us, its main work was fighting in the air. It was equipped for the most part with aeroplanes which were called scouts—not very felicitously, since a scout suggests rather reconnaissance than combat.

These machines carried only one man, were fast, easy to manœuvre, and quick in responding to control. They were armed with one or two machine guns, and they engaged in a form of warfare new in the history of the world, and the most thrilling that can be imagined—for each man fought with his own hand, trusting wholly to his own skill, and that not on his own element, but in outrage of nature, high in the air, surrounded only by the winds and clouds.

The embodiment of the fighting scout squadrons was part of the expansion and organisation of what became the Royal Air Force. Among all the achievements of the war there has been, perhaps, nothing more wonderful than the development of the Royal Flying Corps and the Royal Naval Air Service, and their amalgamation in the great Royal Air Force which fought through the last year of the war. When the war opened, the Royal Flying Corps and the Royal Naval Air Service were bodies of few units, ancillary to the Army and the Navy, of which the control was in the hands of the Army Council and the Board of Admiralty. It was not realised that warfare in the air was a new and distinct type of warfare. Generals who would have laughed at the idea of commanding a fleet, Admirals who would have shrunk from the leadership of an army corps, were quite unconscious of their unfitness to deal with the problems of aerial war. Every step, therefore, of the organisation and expansion of the flying services had to be conducted under the final control of bodies, kindly and sympathetic indeed, but necessarily ignorant. That the Royal Flying Corps attained to its famous efficiency and was expanded more than a hundredfold should earn unforgetting praise for those who were responsible for leading and developing it. The country owes a great debt, which has not, perhaps, been sufficiently recognised, to Sir David Henderson, whose rare gifts of quick intelligence and ready resource must have been taxed to the utmost in his dual position as head of the Flying Corps and member of the Army Council ; to Sir Sefton Brancker, who worked under him in the War Office ; and to Sir Hugh Trenchard, who, from the date that Sir David Henderson came back from France to that of the amalgamation of the flying services in the Royal Air Force, was in command in France. It was the administrative skill of these distinguished men that stood behind the work of the squadrons and made possible their fighting or bombing or reconnaissance. And this background of administrative skill and resource must not be forgotten or suffered to be quite outshone by the brilliant gallantry of the pilots and observers.

But in this book we read, not of the organisation of the Flying Corps or the Air Force, but of the actual work done in the field. We catch glimpses, indeed, of the expansion and organisation which was going on, in the mention of new armament, new machines, new units; and we are able to gauge the importance of the work done at home and at Headquarters in France by the effect produced on the fighting capacity of Squadron No. 60. For example, we hear how machines supplied from France at one point proved untrustworthy in structure, and how the fault was detected and put right. But in the main attention is concentrated on the thrilling story of the achievements of No. 60 against the enemy. I think every reader will agree that he has seldom known a story more moving to the imagination. Many people even now feel apprehensive at flying at all, although familiarity has produced a juster estimate of the degree of risk attending that operation than used to prevail. But to fly and fight, to sit alone in an aeroplane thousands of feet above the ground, to catch sight of an enemy, to go to attack him, flying faster than an express train moves, to venture as near as may be dared, knowing that the slightest collision will cast both helpless to the ground, to dodge and dive and turn and spin, to hide in clouds or in the dazzle of the sun, to fire a machine gun while not losing mastery of the control and rudder of one's aeroplane, to notice the enemy's bullets striking here and there on one's machine, and know that if a bullet hits the engine it means either death or a precarious landing and captivity, and if a bullet hits the petrol tank it means being burned alive in the air, and yet to fight on and, escaping, go forth afresh next day—surely to read of this is to realise with new and penetrating force the stupendous measure of what human skill can do and human courage dare.

The picturesque effect of the fighting is enhanced by the security and comfort in which the pilots rested when they were not in the air, and from which they went up day by day to their terrific duties. Anyone who visited the Flying Corps while the war was going on must have been struck by this poignant contrast. The visitor saw a comfortable mess and billets, roughly organised indeed, but for young men in the height of their strength a pleasant place to live in. Good food and drink, cigarettes to smoke, newspapers to read, and all the fun and merriment that are natural to a group of young men between eighteen and thirty years old. And for most of such squadrons the surroundings seemed peaceful: around were the smiling, highly-cultivated fields of France—perhaps the most evidently civilised country in the world—with nothing to witness of war except the distant booming of its guns. Yet from this abode of youth and ease and joy the dwellers went forth into the abyss of the air, to face danger at which imagination quails and of the reality of which they were grimly reminded by missing week by week some familiar face, gone for ever from their circle. This was what was done and felt by Squadron No. 60, and here is the story of it.

I am sure this book will interest those who read it, but I would have it do something more. Even already the memory of the war is beginning to fade. And it is happy that it should : may its orgy of hate and blood pass from our minds as from our lives ! Yet, while the healing, deadening waters of oblivion are only drawing near, let us save from them with careful hands some jewelled memories, that by them we may be profited ; and, amongst them, this of the men of No. 60, who fought a new warfare with old but unsurpassed courage and found the way of glory among the untrodden paths of air. Many died and many suffered, but they bought for us the unpriced treasure of their example. This is like sunshine to us, giving us life and killing all diseases of the soul. Let us, then, read these pages that we may learn from our hearts to honour the fighting airmen of No. 60, and grow ourselves in honour as we read.

HUGH CECIL.

21 ARLINGTON STREET.
July 1920.

AN ACKNOWLEDGMENT

I⊤ has only been possible to produce this book at all by reason of the help that so many old friends have given me.

My thanks are due to many of them, but in particular to Flight-Lieut. G. W. Dobson, who has himself contributed the account of the squadron at Savy, and has assisted with much of the more arduous work in connection with the preparation of the appendices, which we both hope are now correct in every detail, though we really know quite well that errors will, in fact, be found.

Capt. W. E. Molesworth also has helped very greatly by allowing me to use his vivid letters and by giving the four drawings by himself, which, I venture to think, are of considerable merit. To Mr. R. J. Maclennan, Mr. W. A. H. Newth, and Mr. W. T. Howard, and also to Mr. G. S. Armstrong, father of the late Capt. D. V. Armstrong, perhaps the finest pilot the Flying Corps ever produced, I owe letters and photographs which have been invaluable.

In conclusion, I would ask those many others whom I have not space to mention to believe that I am sincerely grateful for their help.

J. S.

4 WILTON STREET, S.W.1.
June 28, 1920.

CONTENTS

CHAPTER V

CHAPTER VI

APPENDIX I

APPENDIX II

APPENDIX III

APPENDIX IV

LIST OF ILLUSTRATIONS

(Appearing between pages xxiv and 1)

(Appearing between pages 64 and 65)

AN EXPLANATION OF TECHNICAL
TERMS USED

THE line drawing below of a typical tractor biplane will explain to the non-technical reader the meaning of many terms used hereafter which are difficult to describe without the aid of a diagram :

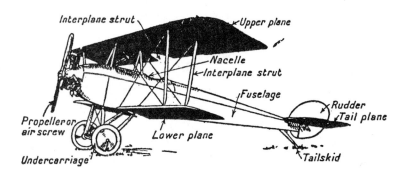

A monoplane has no lower planes, while the top planes sprout from the side of the body like the wings of a bird, but are rigid.

In either type of aeroplane it is the action of the air on the wing surfaces, both upper and lower, when the machine is travelling forward at a minimum speed of about forty miles per hour that keeps it in the air. If the speed is allowed to drop below this minimum (known as the flying speed) the machine "stalls," i.e. becomes uncontrollable, drops its nose and dives to regain flying speed. If this happens near the ground

—within a hundred feet—a serious, and often fatal, crash is the result.

Among the types of aeroplanes used in France during 1916–18, and mentioned in these pages but not described in detail, are :

B.E.2C., R.E.8, AND OTHER TYPES OF TWO-SEATER MACHINES

All two-seater machines carrying one pilot and one observer which were chiefly used for artillery observation, i.e. correcting, by observation from the air, the fire of batteries on the ground.

These were tractor biplanes, i.e. the engine and propeller were in front, while the observer and pilot sat tandem in two cockpits, or nacelles, in the fish-shaped body.

F.E.2B.

A two-seater fighting biplane of the "pusher" type with the engine behind the pilot, who with the observer sat in a cockpit which protruded beyond the leading, or forward, edges of the planes. This aeroplane was used for day and night bombing, for fighting in 1916 and the first half of 1917, and also for reconnaissance and photographic work.

DE HAVILLAND 4

A high-speed tractor two-seater biplane used for bombing, reconnaissance work, and photography.

NIEUPORT, S.E.5, AND SOPWITH CAMEL

Single-seater fighting scouts, all tractor biplanes.

GP. CAPT. A. J. L. SCOTT, CB, MC, AFC. (*via CFS*)

GROUP OF PILOTS AT BOFFLES, SEPTEMBER 1918.
Left to Right: Lts. Orpen, Tennant, Westergaard, Capts. Beck and Rayner.
(via D. W. Warne)

GROUP OF PILOTS IN MARCH, 1918.
Left to Right: Back Row: Lt. Thornton (with 'Hispano'), Lt. Campbell, 2 Lt. Priestley, Capt. H. D. Crompton (with another Sqn. pet dog), Maj. Moore, Lt. Duncan, Lt. Whitney, unknown. *Seated, front:* 2 Lt. Griffith, 2 Lt. Cunningham, Capt. Hammersley, Capt. J. B. Crompton, Lt. Molyneux. *(via D. W. Warne)*

SE 5A E3916 OVERTURNED ON LANDING ON 11 AUGUST, 1918, By 2 Lt. Sinclair
showing the markings used by 'B' Flt. at the time.
(*via D. W. Warne*)

SE 5 A8898 IN AUGUST/SEPTEMBER 1917
when it bore the personalised markings of Capt. 'Grid' Caldwell, OC 'B' Flt. The use of orthochromic film has
disguised the fact the 'B' Flt. used yellow for the white-outlined Sqn. aircraft markings on the fuselage. The
white-topped fin bears the fern emblem of New Zealand.
(*via D. W. Warne*)

AN SE5A WITH 200 H.P. HISPANO SUISA ENGINE, ARMED WITH ONE VICKERS AND ONE LEWIS GUN

SIXTY SQUADRON
R.A.F.
1916 - 1919

SIXTY SQUADRON
R.A.F.

CHAPTER I

THE FORMATION OF THE SQUADRON

To create a new flying unit is a task which entails much thought and labour, and the formation of 60 had been a matter for the careful consideration of the R.F.C. authorities for many months before the squadron number could appear on any of those manifold returns, without a bountiful supply of which no country seems able to go to war. Vital points for preliminary consideration are : The type of aeroplane and the numbers of this type likely to be available in the future ; the engines, and, no less important, the spares which must be procured in adequate quantities if these engines are to be kept in running condition. The training units, too, must be increased in order to keep the new service formation up to strength in pilots. A sufficient number of trained mechanics must be got from somewhere, and these have usually to be wrung from the commanders of other units, themselves already short of trained personnel, and as a rule most reluctant to part with good men.

1

All these matters were at last decided, and 60 Squadron was formed on May 1, 1916. At that time there were in the Royal Flying Corps about thirty-five service squadrons all told, of which by far the greater number were in France. The Royal Naval Air Service had at this date considerably fewer service units. When the Armistice was signed, there were well over two hundred service squadrons in the Royal Air Force, which had come into being as an independent entity distinct from the Army or the Navy on April 1, 1918. During the months previous to the formation of 60, the Germans, with the aid of the Fokker monoplane, which they produced in the autumn of 1915, had begun seriously to interfere with our artillery observation machines. At this period of the war—early 1916—we had no complete single-seater fighting scout squadrons, but achieved the protection of the artillery machines, mostly B.E.2C.s, by having a few Bristol and other scouts in each two-seater squadron.

As a result of these losses, General Trenchard decided to form some new scout squadrons, of which 60 shortly became one, and also to re-equip some of the existing squadrons with scouts. No. 1 Squadron, for example, was given Nieuports (a French machine), at that time the equal of any German fighter.

No. 60 was formed from No. 1 Reserve Aeroplane Squadron at Gosport. Major F. Waldron, known to his friends as " Ferdy," was the first commander of the new unit. He had previously commanded No. 1 R.A.S., and was a cavalry officer who had been seconded from his Hussar regiment (the 19th), some time before the war, to the R.F.C. He was one of the earlier military aviators. He had been an instructor at the Central Flying School at Upavon and was a first-class pilot. The three original flight commanders (Capts. R. Smith-Barry, A. S. M. Somers, and H. C. Tower) were all three old Etonians. The original flying officers were : Capt. D. B. Gray ; Lieuts. H. A. Browning-Paterson, J. N. Simpson, G. F. A. Portal, H. H. Balfour, H. Meintjies, A. D. Bell-Irving ; 2/Lieuts. C. A. Ridley, D. V. Armstrong, H. G. Smart, and G. D. F. Keddie.

The observers were : Lieuts. R. H. Knowles and G. Williams ; 2/Lieuts. L. L. Clark, H. J. Newton, H. H. Harris, H. Good, C. F. Overy, J. I. M. O'Beirne, W. E. G. Bryant, J. Laurie-Reid, J. N. O. Heenan (A.E.O.), and J. Bigood (A.E.O., wireless).

Usually a new squadron received its machines in England at its home station and flew them over to France. 60 Squadron, however, was to be equipped with Moranes, French machines which were not built in England at that time. Consequently the squadron, with its motor transport, stores, etc., crossed to France by sea, and went to St. Omer, where its equipment was completed.

An R.F.C. squadron had two sergeant-majors :

one disciplinary, the other technical. Waldron,
when forming 60, chose these warrant officers with
considerable discretion. Sergt.-Maj. Aspinall, an
old Guardsman brought into the Flying Corps by
Basil Barrington-Kennet in the very early days,
was the disciplinary warrant officer. He had
qualified as a rigger and had tried to learn to fly,
but it was as a disciplinarian that he really shone.
He played no inconsiderable part in the achieve-
ment of whatever success the squadron may have
had. He was a first-class soldier, and his instructions to flight commanders in the form of little
typewritten lectures were gems of their kind. It
should be remembered that at times the casualties
in the squadron were very heavy, and officers
became flight commanders at an age which would
have been regarded as absurd before the war.
" The Great Man," as we called him, would explain
with profound respect to a captain promoted,
most deservedly, at the age of nineteen the
necessity for assuming a judicial demeanour when
an air mechanic was brought up before him on
some minor charge ; he would, further, instruct
the young flight commander most carefully in the
punishments appropriate to each offence, and all
this without in the smallest particular transgress-
ing that code of military etiquette which regulates
so strictly the relations between commissioned and
warrant officers. Only his successive commanding
officers know how much of the tranquillity and
contentment of the men was due to " the Great

Man." The technical sergeant-major, Smyrk by name, was a wizard with an internal combustion engine. He had been employed at the Gramophone Co.'s factory at Hayes in civil life before joining the R.F.C. in 1912, and had a gift for teaching fitters their business. During almost all the war, two fitters a month had to be sent home to assist in the manning of new units, while the squadrons in the field had, in consequence, always to carry a percentage of untrained or partially trained men, who had to be made into experts on the engines with which they were equipped. The technical sergeant-major had to train these men, and was also the specialist who was called in whenever one of the flights had an unusually refractory engine which had baffled both the flight commander and his flight sergeant. Smyrk was always equal to every call upon him, and a long line of pilots should, and no doubt do, remember him with gratitude, for, after all, the degree of efficiency with which the engine was looked after often meant the difference between a landing in Hunland and getting home.

After a few days at St. Omer we received our machines, which were Moranes of three different types: "A" Flight had Morane "bullets," 80 h.p.; "B" Flight, 110 h.p. Morane biplanes; and "C" Flight, Morane "parasols."

Of the "parasol," a two-seater monoplane, it is unnecessary to say very much, as they were soon replaced by "bullets," and "C" Flight did practically no work on them. The machine is best, perhaps, described as a biplane without any bottom planes, by which is meant that the wings were above the pilot's head, a feature which suggested its nickname. It had an 80 h.p. Le Rhone at that time, almost the best air-cooled rotary engine. They were good for artillery registration, as the view downward was excellent ; they were very stable also, easy to fly and to land, and, in fact, were " kind " machines, giving their pilots the sort of feeling afforded by a good-tempered, confidential old hunter.

The Morane biplane had a more powerful engine, the 110 Le Rhone, also an air-cooled rotary, and was quite an efficient " kite," as the R.F.C. called them, with its inveterate habit of inventing pet names for its aeroplanes. It was draughty and cold to sit in, but was light on the controls and had a reasonably good performance. This machine was also a two-seater, like the " parasol," with the observer's seat behind the pilot's.

The Morane "bullet," with a 80 h.p. Le Rhone engine, was quite a different proposition.

This was a monoplane with a fuselage (body) of the monococque, or cigar-shaped, type and very small wings, giving, therefore, a very high loading per square foot of lifting surface. The speed near the ground was not too bad for 1916, being about ninety to ninety-five miles per hour, but, owing to the high loading on the wings, the machine became inefficient at a height. It had the gliding angle of a brick, as a pilot moodily complained after an unsuccessful forced landing. It is obvious that, if a machine has a very small wing surface, it must be kept going fast, when gliding without the engine, to preserve its flying speed, and this can only be done by keeping the nose well down; hence the unfriendly description quoted above.

Above 10,000 feet it was difficult to turn a "bullet" sharply and steeply without "stalling"; moreover, in bad weather it was very uncomfortable to fly, giving the impression that it was trying its best to kill the pilot all the time. The lateral control,[1] of the "warp" type, was to some extent responsible for this. The armament was a fixed Lewis gun firing through the propeller, which was fitted with a metal deflector —a steel wedge which prevented the propeller being shot through. There was no synchronising gear on any of the Moranes. By this is meant the device by which the detonation of the gun was harmonised with the beat of the propeller; actually the gun is blocked when the blades of the propeller are in the line of fire.

Later on we were given some "bullets" with 110 h.p. Le Rhones, but these were no better, as the loading was even higher with the heavier engine, and their performance above 8,000 feet was consequently poor. The climb for the first few thousand feet was wonderful, as the engine seemed almost to pull the machine straight up.

[1] By means of which the machine is tilted sideways.

Generally speaking, the "bullet" was not a success, as it was too difficult to fly for the average pilot. Nevertheless, as several of our pilots, notably Smith-Barry, Gilchrist, Foot, Grenfell, Meintjies, and Hill, and in particular D. V. Armstrong, were considerably above the average, some useful work was accomplished on these machines.

The equipment having been completed, we moved to Boisdinghem, between St. Omer and Boulogne, for a few days' practice with the new machines. This was very necessary, as hardly anyone had flown Moranes before.

On June 10 we were ordered to Vert Galant, an aerodrome astride the Doullens-Amiens road, and joined the 13th Wing of the 3rd Brigade R.F.C., operating with the 3rd Army. War flying was started a few days later, and it at once became apparent that our anti-aircraft batteries found difficulty in distinguishing our "bullets" from the Fokkers. In consequence the black cowls of our machines were painted red to help the "archie" [1] gunners, who had been assiduously firing at 60's machines.

The work at this time chiefly consisted of offensive patrols, which were supposed to keep the air clear for our corps and bombing machines. Numerous reconnaissances were also carried out. In these days scouts usually worked in pairs, but larger formations of five and six machines were becoming more common; later in the war

[1] Anti-aircraft or high-angle guns on the ground.

it was the rule to send out a whole squadron, or as many of its machines as were serviceable, over the line at once ; but in 1916 aeroplanes and pilots were, usually, too scarce to send more than two off the ground at once.

On August 3, 1916, Claude Ridley had a forced landing near Douai through engine failure when dropping a spy over the lines. His adventures were remarkable. His spy got out, told Ridley to hide for a little, and presently, returning with civilian clothes and some money, told him that he must now shift for himself. Ridley did so with such address that he eluded capture for three months on the German side of the line, and eventually worked his way via Brussels to the Dutch frontier and escaped. This was a good performance, none the worse because he could speak neither French nor German. The method he adopted was a simple one—he would go up to some likely-looking civilian and say, " I am a British officer trying to escape; will you help me ?" They always did. He had many interesting adventures. For example, he lay up near the Douai aerodrome and watched the young Huns learning to fly and crashing on the aerodrome ; here he saw one of our B.E.s brought down, and the pilot and observer marched past him into captivity ; later the conductor of a tram in the environs of Brussels suspected him, but, knocking the man down, he jumped into a field of standing corn and contrived to elude pursuit.

This method of landing spies was not popular with R.F.C. pilots, as there was always quite a chance that one might not be able to get the machine off again, and, anyhow, it was a nerve-racking experience to have to land in a field after a necessarily hurried survey from the air, and wait while your spy climbed slowly—very slowly—out. Later, different and, from the pilot's point of view, improved devices were adopted ; the spy was made to sit on the plane with a parachute and to jump off when told. Occasionally they refused to jump, nor is it easy to blame them, so a further improvement is said to have been introduced by which the pilot could pull a lever and drop the wretched agent out through the bottom of the fuselage, after which he parachuted down to earth.

They were very brave men, these French spies who voluntarily entered the occupied territory in this hazardous manner. They were usually dropped either in the late evening or early morning.

CHAPTER II

Sixty had not to wait long for its first taste of serious fighting. The " aerial offensive," which always precedes any " push," was already well developed when the squadron commenced war flying. Casualties were heavy, and on July 3, two days after the official commencement of the Somme battle, Ferdy Waldron was shot down and killed on the " other side." He considered it his duty to try and do one job per day over the line, and on this particular morning he led "A" Flight's 80 h.p. "bullets" over at 4 a.m. in perfect weather. The other members of the patrol were Smith-Barry, Armstrong, Simpson, and Balfour. The last - named thus describes the fight: " Both Armstrong and Simpson fell out, through engine trouble, before we reached Arras. Armstrong landed by a kite balloon section and breakfasted with Radford (Basil Hallam, the actor), whose kite balloon was attacked a few days later, and who met his death through the failure of his parachute. Waldron led the remaining two along the Arras-Cambrai road. We crossed at about 8,000 feet, and just before reaching Cambrai we were about 9,000, when I suddenly saw a large

11

formation of machines about our height coming
from the sun towards us. There must have been
at least twelve. They were two-seaters led by
one Fokker (monoplane) and followed by two
others. I am sure they were not contemplating
' war ' at all, but Ferdy pointed us towards them
and led us straight in.

"My next impressions were rather mixed. I
seemed to be surrounded by Huns in two-seaters.
I remember diving on one, pulling out of the dive,
and then swerving as another came for me. I can
recollect also looking down and seeing a Morane
about 800 feet below me going down in a slow
spiral, with a Fokker hovering above it following
every turn. I dived on the Fokker, who swallowed
the bait and came after me, but unsuccessfully,
as I had taken care to pull out of my dive while
still above him. The Morane I watched gliding
down under control, doing perfect turns, to about
2,000 feet, when I lost sight of it. I thought he
must have been hit in the engine. After an
indecisive combat with the Fokker I turned home,
the two-seaters having disappeared. Smith-
Barry I never saw from start to finish of the
fight. I landed at Vert Galant and reported that
Ferdy had ' gone down under control.' We all
thought he was a prisoner, but heard soon afterwards that he had landed safely but died of
wounds that night, having been hit during the
scrap.

" About twenty minutes after I had landed,

Smith-Barry came back. He had not seen us, but had been fighting the back two Fokkers, which he drove east, but not before he had been shot about by them, one bullet entering the tail and passing up the fuselage straight for his back until it hit the last cross-member, which deflected the course of the missile sufficiently to save him."

This was the end of a first-class squadron commander, and, coming so early in our fighting career, was a heavy blow. If he had lived, Waldron must have made a great name for himself in the R.F.C.

Smith-Barry now took over the squadron. He was a great " character "—an Irishman with all an Irishman's charm. A trifle eccentric, he was a fine pilot. He had crashed badly near Amiens in the retreat from Mons, the first Flying Corps casualty, breaking both his legs, which left him permanently lame. Although beloved by his squadron, his superiors sometimes found him a little trying officially. It is often said, half admiringly, of a man by his friends that " he doesn't care a damn for anyone." I believe this to have been almost literally true of Smith-Barry. He could do anything with an aeroplane, and delighted in frightening his friends with incredible aerial antics. He was a fine, if original, squadron commander, almost too original, in fact, even for the R.F.C., where, if anywhere in the fighting services, originality was encouraged. At a later stage (in 1917) in Smith-Barry's career he rendered a very great service to the Corps and to the country by bringing his contempt for precedent and genius for instruction to bear on the question of teaching pilots to fly.   It is no exaggeration to say that he revolutionised instruction in aviation, and, having been given almost a free hand by General J. Salmond, he organised his Gosport School of Special Flying, which afterwards developed into a station where all flying instructors were trained.

He has been seen to walk down the Strand in full uniform with an umbrella.

When promoted in 1918 to the command of a brigade, he, having come into conflict with authority, dispatched the following telegrams on the same day to his immediate superior : (1) " Am returning to Gosport.   Smith-Barry, Brig.-Gen." (2) " Have arrived at Gosport.   Smith - Barry, Lieut.-Col."

Smith-Barry's batman was a French boy named Doby, a refugee from Lille, whom Nicolson, sometime private secretary to General Seely and one of the early pilots of the R.F.C., had picked up during the retreat from Mons and taken back to England with him.   When Nicolson was killed at Gosport, Smith-Barry appointed Doby as his batman and, in order to take him to France, dressed him in R.F.C. uniform and called him Air Mechanic Doby.   This boy was most useful, being competent to bargain with his compatriots for the goods which the mess required.   When a year had gone by and there had been several changes in command, nobody knew his history, and he was regarded as a genuine member of the Corps. History does not relate how he was eventually " demobilised."

This, then, was the kind of man who took over the squadron on Waldron's death – at a critical point in its career.

Those who were most conspicuous during the battles of the Somme were : Ball (who joined from 11 Squadron in August), Summers and Tower (two of the original flight commanders), Gilchrist, Latta, Grenfell, Meintjies, A. D. Bell Irving, Phillippi, Hill, Foot, Vincent, Armstrong, and Walters. Foot, as one of the most skilful pilots, was given a " Spad," on which he did great execution during the autumn.

The fighting was mainly over places like Bapaume, Courcelette, Martinpuich, Busigny, St. Quentin, Cambrai, Havrincourt, etc.

Ball began to show very prominently about this time, several times destroying two or more hostile aeroplanes, and hardly a day passed without at least one Hun being added to his bag. Much has been written about Albert Ball, so much that at this date it is difficult to add anything of interest to the accounts which are already so widely known; but this at least can confidently be said, that never during the war has any single officer made a more striking contribution to the art of war in the air than he, who was

the first to make what may be called a business of
killing Huns.   He allowed nothing to interfere
with what he conceived to be the reason of his
presence in an aeroplane in France—the destruction of the enemy wherever and whenever he
could be found.   He was a man—a boy in truth—
of a kindly nature, possessed by a high sense of
duty and patriotism.   These months (August and
September 1916) saw Ball at his best, and though
it is true that he was awarded the Victoria Cross
after his death in an heroic fight in the spring of
1917, when he was a flight commander in 56
Squadron, yet it was in the summer and autumn
of 1916 in 11 and 60 Squadrons that he began to
show the Flying Corps what fighting in the air
really meant.   The copy of a report rendered to
R.F.C. H.Q. is given below :

   " Lieut. Ball has had more than twenty-five
combats since May 16 in a single-seater scout.
   " Of these thirteen have been against more than
one hostile machine.
   " In particular, on August 22, he attacked in
succession formations of 7 and 5 machines in the
same flight ; on August 28, 4 and 10 in succession ;
on August 31, 12.
   " He has forced 20 German machines to land,
of which 8 have been destroyed—1 seen to be
descending vertically with flames coming out of
the fuselage, and 7 seen to be wrecked on the
ground.

" During this period he has forced two hostile balloons down and destroyed one.

"(*Sgd.*) J. F. A. HIGGINS,

" *Brigadier-General,*

" *Commanding 3rd Brigade R.F.C.*

" IN THE FIELD,

"*Sept.* 1, 1916."

Of the others, Latta became a wonderful pilot; Gilchrist, a gallant South African, commanded 56 at the end of the war and became one of the very best instructors under Smith-Barry at Gosport; Roderick Hill, a fine pilot, is also an artist of no small reputation; A. D. Bell Irving worthily upheld the traditions of an heroic Canadian family whose name will always appear prominently in any history of the Air Force; while Meintjies, also a South African, though young, himself displayed an infinite patience, together with a wisdom far beyond his years, in the introduction of new pilots to the hazardous game of aerial fighting as practised on the Western Front, of which he himself was a first-class exponent.

As for D. V. Armstrong, a South African, who was killed in a crash just as the war had ended, and who after leaving 60 became a brilliant night-flying pilot, the following letter from Col. Small will give some slight idea of the work done by him in 151 Night Fighting Squadron.

" At 10.40 on the night of September 17/18, whilst on patrol east of Bapaume, Capt. Arm-

2

strong observed a Gotha biplane caught in a concentration of searchlight at 8,500 feet, with a Camel machine behind it.

" Seeing the Camel was not engaging the E.A. (enemy aeroplane) from a sufficiently close range, this officer dived down, coming in on the E.A.'s right. He closed right up under its tail and fired 100 rounds into it. The E.A. then burst into flames and dived to the ground, where it burst into pieces just east of Bapaume.

" On the night of September 10/11, 1918, on receipt of a report that E.A. was over the 4th Army front, Capt. Armstrong volunteered to go up, although the weather was practically impossible for flying, the wind blowing at about fifty miles an hour, accompanied by driving rain storms. In spite of this, Capt. Armstrong remained on his patrol 1 hour 5 minutes, although his machine was practically out of control on several occasions. On landing, his machine had to be held down to prevent it being blown over.

" On the night of August 6/7, 1918, Capt. Armstrong attacked Estrées-en-Chaussée acrodrome. After dropping three Cooper bombs on the hangars from 600 feet, he observed an E.A. coming in to land. Capt. Armstrong then closed under the E.A.'s tail and opened fire from fifteen yards' range when at 700 feet. The E.A.'s observer answered the fire, and then suddenly ceased altogether. Capt. Armstrong continued firing until the E.A. suddenly turned to the right with nose down and crashed on its aerodrome, bursting into flames as it struck the ground. This officer then dropped his fourth bomb on the wreck and fired a further burst into it, returning to his aerodrome with all ammunition expended.

" On the night of August 8/9, 1918, although the clouds were at about 500 feet, this officer flew to the same hostile aerodrome, but finding no activity there and seeing no lights whatever, he flew to Cizancourt Bridge, dropping his four bombs upon it from 500 feet.

" On this night he was unable at any period to fly at over 800 feet, owing to low driving clouds and a very strong wind.

" Capt. Armstrong attacked aerodromes as follows on the dates shown :

" MOISLANS, 3.15 a.m. to 3.30 a.m. on August 21/22, 1918, dropping two incendiary and two Cooper bombs from 400 feet on hutments and tents, although subjected to the most accurate and fierce machine-gun fire from the ground and his machine being brightly illuminated in the glare of the incendiary bombs.

" ESTRÉES-EN-CHAUSSÉE, on the night of July 31—August 1, 1918, dropping four bombs on landing lights from 500 feet.

" Capt. Armstrong took part in the defence of London against all but three raids by E.A. between September 1917 and June 1918.

" This officer has been the right hand of his squadron commander since the formation of his squadron, and has, by his wonderful flying, taught the pilots of 151 Squadron more than any other instructor could possibly have done. He has demonstrated to all pilots daily the only successful method of attack at night against E.A. by personal supervision of their flying.

"As a flight commander I cannot speak too highly of him and his wonderful spirit at all times. His bravery as a pilot at all times and in all weather conditions cannot be surpassed, and I am unable to recommend him too strongly for this decoration.

"B. C. D. SMALL,
"*Lieut.-Colonel,*
"*Commanding* 54 *Wing R.A.F.*

"*Sept.* 19, 1918."

It was about this time that " balloon strafing " was invented by Headquarters. Three Le Prieur rockets of the ordinary type were attached to the interplane struts on each wing; these were fired by means of an electric bell-push in the nacelle (or pilot's seat), and if they hit the hostile kite balloon, were guaranteed to send it down in flames. The effect of this extra load was to make the machine singularly unhandy when fighting, but it must be admitted that they did effectually set hostile kite balloons alight if the pilot was sufficiently resolute to restrain himself from pressing the button until he was within 150 yards of the object balloon. This sounds much easier than, in fact, it was, as hostile balloons were usually found as low as 2,500 feet, and the wretched pilot had to contend with heavy gunfire from the ground, while always remembering that he was some considerable distance over the line and had sacrificed his height in order to approach the balloon. The aeroplane of those days would glide about one mile per 1,000 feet in still air, and, remembering that the balloons were usually at least two miles behind the line and that the wind was almost always from the west, it will be obvious that, if the engine was hit, there was very little chance of gliding back over the trenches. Hence it will be readily understood that balloon strafing was not enormously popular among junior flying officers.

Nevertheless, Gilchrist, Bell Irving, Summers, Phillippi, and Hill all successfully brought down hostile kite balloons during the Somme battles (September 1916).

Later, in 1917, Buckingham incendiary ammunition was used for destroying balloons. This change was greatly appreciated by the R.F.C., because the handiness of the machine was not impaired, as was the case when the Le Prieur rockets were carried.

From Vert Galant the squadron moved to St. André on August 3, 1916, to refit, having only five pilots left. There the first flight of Nieuport scouts was received and, after a fortnight, another move was ordered to Izel le Hameau on August 16. This was an aerodrome we were destined to occupy again during the Arras battle. We here became a homogeneous unit completely equipped with Nieuport scouts, and moved three miles away to Savy, midway between Arras and St. Pol, early in September. Here, during November, little flying was possible owing to continual rain and fog, and the squadron settled down, almost in the Roman manner, into winter-quarters. Savy Aerodrome stood just above the village of that name, and while " C " Flight were accommodated in huts on the aerodrome so as to be near their machines in order to deal quickly with any Huns who were bold enough to cross the line, the remainder of the squadron were billeted in the Mayor's château in the village itself, some half a mile away. Here pigs and turkeys were kept, out of which the mess made a good profit, and which, in addition, provided both an excellent Christmas dinner for the men and the material for the farewell banquet to Smith-Barry, who was posted to Home Establishment early in December. This dinner was somewhat memorable. The guests included General Higgins (the brigade commander), Pretyman (the wing commander), Col. Lewis and Barnaby of the " archie " gunners, Robert Loraine and several other squadron commanders. The squadron band, organised by Vincent, performed during dinner with great vigour. Led by Sergt. Nicod at the piano and conducted by Vincent himself, it helped to enliven the evening very considerably.

In addition to the band, the squadron ran at

this period both a Rugby and an Association football team. The Rugby side was for a time invincible, the leading players being Middlemas, the wing machine-gun officer, an old Cambridge Blue and a fine three-quarter ; D. Bell Irving and Giles, a first-class pair of halves ; and Meintjies, a tower of strength at full back. The Soccer team also won many matches, captained by the " Great Man," Sergt.-Maj. Aspinall ; while the stores sergeant, a league player, was the star performer at centre-forward. Matches were very difficult to arrange, as they had to be postponed if the weather was fine, and could only take place, therefore, on thoroughly " dud " days, to use the inevitable R.F.C. expression.

Smith-Barry was succeeded by Major E. P. Graves, a regular gunner, young in years, who had crashed a Gnome Martinsyde scout at Netheravon early in 1915 and spent many months in hospital, emerging towards the end of that year permanently lame but quite fit to fly. He had been staff captain and brigade major to General Higgins at home when recovering from his injuries, but as soon as he became fit gave his General no peace until he was allowed to go to France in a fighting unit. He got posted to 20 Squadron as a flight commander early in 1916, and had been sent home again on promotion to command a training squadron after six months of very good work in France. Soon after he had taken over, the squadron was moved from Savy back to Izel le

Hameau, the correct name of the station being Filescamp Farm. Here, with the aid of the local R.E. and thanks to Graves's tireless efforts, an almost ideal little station was created in the orchard adjoining the great grey walls of M. Tetus's demesne. This was a very old and picturesque house, half farm and half château, and was removed some two miles from a main road or railway line, a circumstance which prevented the aerodrome being bombed at night for a very long time, as it was hard to see from the air. An admirable mess, with a large brick fireplace, corrugated-iron hangars, together with Nissen huts for the officers and N.C.O.s and good accommodation for the men, were all built by the sappers. At this station in M. Tetus's orchard the squadron found a quiet retreat when not actually engaged with the enemy. It is, perhaps, appropriate here to observe that every pilot at this time did, on the average, three patrols in two days over the line, and seldom returned to the aerodrome without a brush of some kind with the Boche. The contrast between our quarters and those occupied by the infantry and gunners in the line was striking. We had cream at every meal, and a hot bath—made by digging an oblong hole in the turf and lining it with a waterproof sheet—whenever we felt inclined. That the mess was good was largely due to Dobson, a 19th Hussar, partly paralysed as the result of a fall when riding in a steeplechase before the war, who was the recording officer at this time, having vainly tried to qualify as an observer in spite of his disability.

During the early months of 1917 there was a very hard frost, which made it difficult for the Germans to start their engines, most of which were water-cooled stationaries, but did not affect 60's air-cooled rotaries, though both sides found that their machine guns were almost useless owing to the extreme cold. This frost lasted till mid-February.

Below will be found the first of a series of letters written by Molesworth, who joined the squadron at this time. They have been inserted as far as possible whenever the narrative reaches the events which they describe.

> " 60 Squadron R.F.C.,
> " B.E.F., France.
> "*March* 1917.

" It has been snowing hard all day, so at last I have a chance of sending you a scrawl.

" Well! old bean, I had my first trip with my flight commander over the lines on the 2nd. My word! it was some trip too, I can tell you. I was posted to ' A ' Flight and allotted a machine. Having interviewed my C.O. with much fear and trembling, I was told that he would take me up to the lines to have a look round. My job was to watch and follow my leader, look out for any Huns and get a good idea of the ground. By this time I had got well acquainted with my machine, or ' grid,'[1] as it was generally called by one of our Colonial flight commanders, and felt quite confident that, if we met any Huns, I could give them a pretty hot time.

" We started off late in the afternoon, climbing to about 8,000 feet. The view was wonderful — the ground covered with a thin coating of snow, while far away one could see the incessant flashing of the guns near the battered old town of Arras. White clouds floated in the ground mist over the eastern horizon like great icebergs, their tops tinged with a wonderful pink which one only sees in the air.

" I shall never forget that first impression of the battle-field from an aeroplane ; it was so different to the sights of war on the ground. No Huns were on view, but a few of our artillery machines were still working. We turned home and landed in the dusk.

"I don't think I told you about a Boche we brought down last week. We got him quite near the aerodrome —apparently he had lost his way in the clouds. He appeared out of them at about 3,000 feet over our heads. Of course, every available machine dashed off in pursuit, and caught him up in a few minutes, as he was forced to turn from the lines by some old F.E. Birds.[2]

---

[1] All flying machines were known as " grids " in the squadron.

[2] The F.E.8 was a " pusher " machine, that is with the engine and propeller behind the pilot. It was used for reconnaissance work at this time, but later became one of our night-bombing aeroplanes.

They all went for him, and he had to land in a ploughed field near-by. He put the machine down quite well, without crashing anything, but one of his pursuers, who belonged to the squadron next to us, turned upside down in his excitement when landing. However, he did not hurt himself, and managed to prevent the Hun from setting his machine on fire, by holding a Very pistol [1] at his head.

" Afterwards I had a chat with the prisoner in French, and found out that he was a star pilot, having a number of our machines to his credit and the inevitable Iron Cross.

" I am all out for getting a Hun now, and hope to be able to tell you, when I next write, that my name has appeared in *Comic Cuts*." [2]

The Nieuport scout deserves a short description, as it was on the successive types of this aeroplane that nearly a year's work was done, from September 1916 to July 1917. This single-seater fighter was a French machine, and one of the most successful in its day which our allies ever produced. The various types of this make with which the squadron was at different times equipped—15, 16, 17, 21, 24, and 29—showed a continuous improvement in performance, though all had the same

[1] Used for signals. It fired a kind of cartridge from which a flaming ball was discharged of red, green, or white lights.

[2] The weekly official record of work done by the R.F.C., including all scraps in which the Hun " crashed " or " went down out of control."

engine, 110 h.p. Le Rhone, which itself was modified slightly and converted into a 120 h.p. engine by the substitution of aluminium for cast-iron pistons. Through all the modifications introduced in each successive type the machine preserved its essential characteristics. It was a biplane, but its lower planes were non-lifting and only operated to stabilise the machine to some extent in flight ; the top planes were streamlined with the pilot's eyes, giving him the free view which is essential in a fighting scout. It may be said that it was mainly this characteristic, that it was good to see out of, that made the Nieuport, in 1916, the best fighting machine on either side. Strong in construction and very handy, it could turn inside any German aeroplane we ever encountered. It was not very fast, but, with an exceptionally good climb to 10,000 feet, it was no bad " grid " on which to go Hun-hunting between the sea and the Somme. It was armed with a single Lewis gun carrying a double drum with ninety rounds of ·303 ammunition and two spare drums. The gun was mounted on the top plane and fired over the propeller at an angle slightly above the horizontal. The earlier Nieuports were all treated with a bright silver-coloured " dope " —the substance used to tighten the fabric— and when properly turned out had a very smart appearance.

Another characteristic of all types was the V-shaped interplane strut, which, although the

Germans also used them in their D3 Albatros, made the machines easy to recognise in the air.

In conclusion, the Silver Nieuport was a good machine to fight in, but a bad one either for running away or for catching a faint-hearted enemy, as its best air speed, even near the ground, rarely exceeded ninety-six or ninety-seven miles per hour.

CHAPTER III

ARRAS

WITH the beginning of March 1917, the Boche became very active in the air. The D3 V-strut Albatros appeared in numbers on the 3rd Army front, and about the same time a squadron of red-painted machines of this type, known to the R.F.C. as " the Circus," did a good deal of damage to British machines and annoyed us very much. One aeroplane in particular, called the " Pink Lady " on account of an absurd story that it was flown by a woman—the machine itself was coloured bright red—was often seen between Arras and Albert. It is thought that the pilot was Freiherr von Richthofen the elder. This machine it was that, venturing well over our side of the line on March 6, 1917, crashed an F.E. and went on and engaged and shot down Evelyn Graves, whose machine caught fire. When picked up, he was found to have been shot through the head, so that he was spared the pain of death by burning.

After Evelyn Graves's death, A. J. L. Scott, of the Sussex Yeomanry, was appointed to succeed him. He was a flight commander in 43—a Sopwith two-seater squadron—and was also lame as the result of a crash during the early part of the

war, being the third lame squadron commander
in succession appointed to 60.

Scott took up his appointment on March 10,
1917, about the time that the aerial offensive
precedent to the Arras battle began to develop.

There had been, on the 3rd Army front, a lull
during January and February, and by a lull is
meant that pilots were doing one job a day instead
of the two that they were almost certain to be
called upon for when business was good. The
casualties lists show this clearly, as, though E. O.
Grenfell and Gilchrist were wounded in December,
there were only two more casualties until Evelyn
Graves's death in March—R. Hopper, killed on
January 11; and E. G. Herbert, wounded on the
28th. February passed without the loss of a
single officer. This was due mainly to the month
of hard frost referred to above, which kept the
Hun machines on the ground. Even when
machines did meet in the air at this time, it was
very difficult to get the guns to fire, so that on
several occasions the pilots, after manœuvring
round one another for a while, waved hands and
went home. A non-freezing gun-oil was brought
out before the next winter, which put an end to
these not altogether unwelcome interludes to the
sterner business. Mention of Grenfell's wound
calls to mind the occasion on which he received it.
An O.P. (offensive patrol) led by him, and con-
sisting of Caldwell, Daly, Whitehead, Weedon,
and Meintjies, met a two-seater Albatros over

Dainville on our side of the line.   All our machines
opened fire, and the Hun hurriedly landed.   Grenfell, anxious to get down and claim him, crashed
and broke his leg, while all the other five machines
landed, and three of these also crashed, not so
seriously as to injure the pilots, but enough to
prevent them taking off again.   Thus the Hun in
one field was flanked by a crashed Nieuport in
every adjoining enclosure, while, to make matters
worse, the Boche observer—who, unlike the pilot,
was not wounded—set fire to his machine to
prevent it falling into our hands.   The machine
shortly exploded, seriously injuring the observer
and several of our own infantry who by that time
were standing by.   If these had grasped the
situation a little more quickly they could easily
have prevented the destruction of the machine,
which it was important to preserve.

The battle of Arras, as it came to be called,
was now imminent, and would probably have
commenced before April 10 but for an unexpected
move on the part of the enemy.   On March 30,
the first clear day after a spell of bad weather,
the first patrol to land reported thirty or forty
fires in the tract of country east of the Arras-
Albert sector.   Every village for ten or fifteen
miles back was alight.   At first we could not
understand what it meant—for although an
R.F.C. squadron knew a good deal more of what
was happening than a battalion in the line, still
we did not always fully comprehend the meanings

of the incidents we reported, which the G.H.Q. Intelligence Staff could, no doubt, interpret with the help of reports from their numerous other sources of information.

The German retreat of March 14 came, therefore, as a complete surprise to us. For, even at this stage of the war, we had become so used to hearing that the enemy's *morale* was undermined, and that their troops were unwilling to fight, etc., that we had ceased to take much notice of these stories, the truth of which—for they were true — only became manifest nineteen months later.

The next two days, the 14th and 15th, were days of stormy weather, in spite of which patrols were continually sent out to try and ascertain the depth of the withdrawal and to locate the new German positions. The rough-and-ready way in which this was done was to fly low until we came under fire from anti-aircraft guns or rifles and machine guns on the ground. Molesworth, in a letter, gives quite a graphic account of this retreat as follows :

> "60 SQUADRON R.F.C.,
> "B.E.F., FRANCE.
> "*March* 1917.

" No luck for me in the Hun line yet, although the beggars seem to be running on the ground all right.

" Three of us went out the other day, and had the most hectic time. The clouds were about 3,000 feet and very dense, with gaps here and

3

there. We crossed the lines and expected to get
it pretty hot from Archie,[1] but, strangely enough,
nothing happened. Heading towards Croisille,
we came out of a thick cloud and saw a most
extraordinary sight. For miles around every
village was a blazing mass with smoke columns,
like great water-spouts, ascending upwards to
the clouds. Along the roads one could see lines
of retreating men making for the Hindenburg
defences, which we could plainly distinguish
owing to the amount of barbed wire entangle-
ments round them. Suddenly we were met by a
perfect tornado of bursting 'archies,' and so were
forced to turn into a cloud. This cloud was so
thick that we all promptly proceeded to lose
ourselves. I looked at my compass[2] and saw
that it was pointing west, so carried on. At last,
after about half an hour's flying, I found myself
alone in an opening in the clouds. Below me
were dozens of shell-holes filled with water ;
round about, black clouds and sheets of driving
rain. I knew I was somewhere near the lines,
and yet could not decide in which direction to
turn. Trusting to the compass I still pushed on
west, and at last the shell-holes disappeared.
Just as my petrol was giving out I spotted some
hangars. There was nothing for it, so I decided
to land. Coming down to about 200 feet I did a

[1] Anti-aircraft guns or shells.
[2] It is very difficult to fly by compass in clouds for any length
of time.

half-circle to get into the wind, and to my utter
disgust saw a large party of Germans on the
ground. I therefore made up my mind that it
must be a Hun aerodrome. No machines were
out, owing to the ' dud ' weather, so I landed,
jumped out of the machine, seized the Very
pistol, and was just going to fire it into the grid
when I saw, to my amazement, two mechanics in
khaki coming across to give me a hand. I tell
you, I have never been so bucked to see anyone
in khaki before. Evidently the party I had seen
were German prisoners. When the old kite
had been filled up I pushed off again, and got
home after about an hour's run. On arrival I
heard that the other two had lost themselves as
well, but had managed to get back. In future I
shall take jolly good care to get to know the
country better before playing about in clouds."

On the 17th and 18th the weather became too
bad to fly, and an " excursion " was organised
in tenders to the nearest points of the old front line,
Ransart and Monchy-au-Bois, near Adinfer Wood ;
this last-named had been the home of a peculiarly
accurate enemy " archie " gun for many months
past. At the latter place skeletons of French
soldiers still hung in the wire, where they had
been since September 1915 at least.

The systematic and deliberate devastation of
the evacuated country made a great impression
on all our pilots, who were also thrilled to see the

very trenches which the enemy's troops had occupied only a few days earlier. It seemed wonderful to see the marks in the muddy sides of the trenches made by German feet and elbows, and the clips of rifle cartridges laid on the fire steps by their sentries less than a week before. Absorbingly interesting, too, to explore their dugouts, and to trace the routes by which their troops came up into the line from the rest billets behind. All the roads had been blown up, and every house in each abandoned village was most efficiently destroyed, except in a few cases, like Bapaume town hall, where delay action mines had been prepared.

One of the most impressive sights was the German cemetery, which was to be found in almost every hamlet, carefully laid out and extremely carefully tended, with monuments, cement steps, and ornamental shrubs symmetrically disposed amid the ruins of the houses among which it stood.

There were souvenirs enough for an army, let alone a squadron, and we were fortunate when collecting them not to fall into a single " booby trap," such as a helmet which exploded when picked up. This expedition is also described by Molesworth in another letter:

" 60 SQUADRON R.F.C.,
"B.E.F., FRANCE.
" *March* 1917.

" The rumour about leave is true, so my turn ought to come in a few days as my name is next

on the list. The weather has been hopeless
lately for aviation. Yesterday some of us
decided to go and have a look at the old Boche
trenches. We chose the ones west of Adinfer
Wood, as they were less likely to be mined than
those further north.

"Having seized a tender, we pushed off after
breakfast towards the line. We got to our front
trenches at about ten o'clock, and left the tender
here, as the road was still in pretty bad repair.
No Man's Land was dotted about with shell-
holes. A few broken stumps of trees lined the
road—war-worn veterans that had stood the test
of battle. (Amongst other souvenirs, I am
bringing you back a walking-stick made from a
branch of one of these.) There was a wood, or
what remained of it, to our right front, as this
part of the line had been very quiet, and was
nothing compared to the utter desolation of the
Somme or ' Arras ' battle-fields.

"The German system of trenches consisted of
thick belts of barbed wire, behind which was a
trench about 10 feet deep, with platforms and
machine-gun emplacements to shoot from.
About every 50 yards or so square openings led
down to the underground dugouts. The old
Hun seems to have lived fairly comfortably, as
there were beds and tables here and there, with
store-rooms and passages connecting each dugout.

"We went about collecting souvenirs very

gingerly, as warnings of booby traps were posted up everywhere we went. But luckily no one was caught out. We managed to collect some tin hats, bombs, Very pistols, and a few other odds and ends, which we loaded into the tender.

" I am bringing some of these home.

" Orders have just come through for us to go on another balloon strafe, so I will finish this when we come back if old Fritz doesn't stop me.

" (*Two hours later*)

" Here I am back again, with a Hun and a ' sausage '[1] added to my bag. I am fearfully bucked with life, as the Major has just told me that I have been made a ' flight commander.' No time for any more, as I am just off to have a cheery time with the other lads, who seem to have done pretty well too."

That the enemy knew that the British intended to attack was evident, because the numbers of the aforementioned V-strut Albatros scouts had obviously increased on this front. The performance of these machines was considerably better than the Nieuport, and they had two Spandau guns firing through the propeller; and, moreover, the circus of red machines led, so they said, by Richthofen, was functioning freely throughout the month of March 1917. It is perhaps unnecessary to repeat that the offensive in the air com-

---

[1] Kite balloon.

mences always before the push on the ground,
and though the latter was timed to commence on
April 10, 60 had a hard month to go through
before this date arrived. We were short of
scout squadrons at this time, and though 48,
the first Bristol fighter squadron, and 56, another
new squadron equipped with the S.E.5s, had
arrived from England, these were to be kept as a
surprise for the Boche, and were not to cross the
line until " zero day," as the day fixed for the
first assault was called. With 56 Ball had come
out again from England, and it was during this
battle that he was killed, on May 7, 1917, after
a severe engagement in which Meintjies, who also
had been posted to 56 after a period of rest
at home, was badly wounded ; the latter is one
of the best pilots, and almost the most popular
officer, 60 ever had.

The flight commanders at this time, mid-
March 1917, were : K. L. Caldwell, who when on
leave fell sick and did not return till June. He
was a New Zealander, a great friend of Meintjies,
and was beloved by everyone. He was a curious
instance of a fine and fearless fighter, but a bad
shot at this time, who in consequence did not
get many Huns ; he afterwards remedied this
defect and made a great reputation both in 60 and
when commanding 74 in 1918. The other two
were Alan Binnie, an Australian who had fought
with the 9th Division in Gallipoli, and Black, who
went sick and was subsequently posted away.

At the beginning of this month (on the day before Graves's death, to be exact) W. A. Bishop joined. The son of a well-known family in Montreal, he had passed through the Royal Military College and had joined the Canadian Cavalry, coming over with his regiment with the first Canadian contingent. On arrival in England he very soon applied to join the Flying Corps, and was posted as an observer to No. 7 Squadron. After a tour of duty in France in this capacity he went home to learn to fly, and was posted to us almost as soon as he had got his wings.

It was curious to notice how quick the mechanics of the squadron were to recognise Bishop's quality. Only a few days after his arrival at the squadron the sergeants gave a musical evening to which the officers were invited, and it was observed that one of the very few toasts which were proposed by them was that of Bishop's health, although at this time he had only destroyed one enemy machine, and none of his fellow-officers had, as yet, any idea of the brilliant career that was in store for him. This occasion, on which he got his first Hun, was remarkable for the fact that his engine failed, and forced him to land very near the front-line trenches. He only, in fact, just succeeded in scraping over. The failure of the engine was due to his inexperience in allowing it to choke while diving. Having landed in a very unhealthy spot, he got rapidly into a dugout occupied by some field gunners, and, with their help, moved his machine every half-hour to prevent the German artillery shelling it. During the night he borrowed a toothbrush from the gunner officer, and with this contrived to clean the sparking plugs of his engine. Having heard nothing of him, the squadron had already reported him missing, when he succeeded in getting a telephone message through to say that he was safe.

Our Corps machines, the eyes of the artillery, were being shot down every day in the valley of the Scarpe, despite our efforts and those of 29 (also with Nieuports) and 11, an F.E.2B. squadron. The ground on both sides of the river was littered with B.E.s. The scouts, whose losses were much heavier, fell usually far over the lines in hostile territory.

The work at this time still consisted mainly of offensive patrols (whose business it was to operate east of the artillery machines and to keep the air clear of hostile scouts), reconnaissances, and sometimes escorts to bombing and photographic patrols. On April 7 M. B. Knowles, C. S. Hall, and G. O. Smart—the latter was originally an N.C.O. pilot who had but lately been commissioned for gallantry in the Field—all failed to return after an engagement with a much superior force of the enemy. At this time it was very hard to get all the photographs wanted by the army owing to the enemy's activity in the air, and when special information about some point was required, 60 was sometimes given the job of taking the photographs. It was thought that the Huns would not expect a scout to be doing photography, and they were not over-keen, even at that time, on attacking a scout formation. It was no easy task this, to fly a sensitive single-seater, look out for Huns, and expose plates at the same time, but it was done with some measure of success. Here follows Molesworth's description of a fight:

"60 Squadron R.F.C.,
"B.E.F., France.
"*April* 1917.

" A Hun at last !

" We started out this morning, led by our new squadron commander, who seems one of the best. Our late C.O. was brought down in flames, this side of the lines, in a scrap. He was a very great loss to the squadron, and we buried him, with full military honours, in a little village cemetery near-by.

" There were five of us on the patrol, my position being the rear one on the left. We got to the lines at about 10,000 feet, and crossed them, making towards Douai. Soon we sighted a small patrol of Sopwith [1] two-seaters, north-east of Arras, flying towards the lines as hard as they

---

[1] These machines were some of the first to be used for recon-naissance purposes. They did about ninety miles an hour " all out," and were therefore difficult to handle against the faster Albatros. It is very often the duty of reconnaissance machines not to engage in a fight, as their news may be lost.

could go, with a large pack of Huns chasing them. The latter managed to get the last machine in flames, the poor devils going down burning like a furnace.

"The Major immediately dived for the Huns, and I knew that I was in for my first real big scrap. The leader saw us coming, and turned east with his nose well down; however, we soon caught him up and started scrapping. Then ensued the usual dog-fight.[1] I managed to get well behind a Hun two-seater which was a little way out of the scrap. He didn't seem to mind me plugging him a bit, and went calmly on. In my excitement I lost my head, and started spinning madly to the ground. Coming out, I saw an Albatros scout[2] about 50 yards ahead, so loosed off at him and saw him spin[3] and crash on the ground, much to my delight.

"Having lost the rest of the formation[4] I headed for home, and found out, on landing, that we had accounted for three Huns. The two-seater which I had been trying to worry was known as the 'Flying Pig,' owing to the likeness of the observer to that rotund animal.

[1] When every machine gets mixed up in a sort of mêlée.

[2] Either of the D3 or D5 type, which was generally used by the enemy at this time. It was an efficient machine for speed, but could not climb as well as our scouts.

[3] A machine is spinning when it is diving towards the ground turning in a corkscrew fashion.

[4] Most fighting is now done in "formation," that is in an organised pack. Either the machines fly in the shape of a wedge or a diamond, or in some order which is most convenient to the "leader."

" Talking about casualties, we have had a pretty hot time the last few days. However, twenty Huns have been accounted for during this time, and many more sent down out of control,[1] so we hope to put up a record in the R.F.C."

From the last week in March to the last week in May our losses were very severe (see Appendix II); in fact, counting those who went sick and those injured in crashes on our side of the line, we lost thirty-five officers during these eight weeks, almost twice the strength of the squadron, which consisted of eighteen pilots and the squadron commander. One week-end in April, the 14th, 15th, and 16th, was especially unlucky, as on Saturday " A " Flight went out six machines strong (full strength) and only one returned. Binnie was leading, and was hit in the shoulder when trying to extricate two of his patrol from a cloud of enemies. The blood from his wound spurted all over the nacelle, obscuring the instruments, and in addition his machine caught fire. He extinguished the flames and then fainted when gliding homeward. The machine must have turned west after this, for he woke up in a little park in Lens, having hit the ground while still

[1] It is very often impossible to watch a machine after it has been hit until it " crashes." It is, therefore, counted as out of control. Sometimes this was used as a " blind " by some pilots to escape. They simply let the machine do what it liked, and when near the ground took control again.

unconscious, without further serious injuries.
He lost his arm at the shoulder, and was a prisoner
till the spring of 1918, when he was repatriated,
and immediately commenced flying again. He
was a very great loss to the squadron, as he was
a first-class flight commander, who had already
destroyed several Huns and would have got a lot
more. On the next day, Sunday, " B " Flight,
five strong, lost two pilots : one, Milot, a French-
Canadian Major, who was killed ; the other,
Hervey, who had already gained two Military
Crosses as an observer and promised very well,
was forced to land on the other side by anti-
aircraft fire. On this patrol Bishop, who had just
been promoted captain, got two Huns and a
balloon, having had five or six combats. On
Monday " C " Flight (Bishop's) went out without
the flight commander, and only one, Young,
returned ; this meant that in three days ten out
of eighteen pilots were lost, and had to be replaced
from England by officers who had never flown
this particular type of machine, because there
were none in England. Our new machines were
collected from Paris, and the chance of a trip to
fly one back was eagerly looked forward to by
every pilot. Some of these new machines were
not well built, and began—to add to our troubles
—to break up in the air. Lieut. Grandin's fell
to bits while diving on a hostile two-seater,
though this may have been due to injury from
machine-gun fire. Caffyn's and Brackenbury's

collapsed when practising firing at ground targets on the aerodrome, and the former was killed; while Ross's wings folded upwards when pulling out of a dive after firing a burst; he was badly injured, but has since recovered. A good show was that put up by Penny, who, when his left lower plane came off while diving on a Hun, contrived to fly the machine back and to land at one of our aerodromes, and quietly reported to the squadron commander as follows: " My lower plane came off, so I thought I had better land. Sorry I left the patrol, sir." The reason for these accidents was that badly seasoned wood was being used by the French manufacturers, who also allowed a lot of little screws to be inserted in the main spars, thus weakening them considerably. H.Q. were informed and the matter was put right.

During this battle the R.F.C. began to take a hand in the ground operations by machine-gunning support troops during an attack. " C " Flight led by Fry, who was given an M.C. for this, did well on May 11, by shooting up the enemy in a cutting east of the chemical works at Roeux, in the valley of the Scarpe. These pilots came back, having exhausted their ammunition, refilled with petrol and 300 rounds, and dashed off again to the chemical works without waiting for orders. One of them, E. S. Howard, who was killed seven days later on an escort to machines doing photography, thus described this adventure :

" On Friday night the infantry made an attack east of Fampoux and we were told off to assist them. When they went over the top, we dived down and emptied our machine guns into the Hun trenches. Our people put up a wonderful barrage; it was good to see, but not at all nice to fly over, as the bursts from the shells threw the machines about. We have just come back from a show, chased four Huns away over their lines, and then flew round keeping our eye on them so they could not come back."

This " low flying," as it was called, became more popular with the higher command, though not with the pilots, as the war went on, and in fact, during the German offensive of March 1918, it was said to have very materially helped to stop the Boche advance on the 5th and 3rd Army fronts.

Hostile balloons also were constantly attacked during April and May, and Bishop, Ross, Molesworth, and Penny did considerable execution. Others who were doing well at this time were Langwill, Hall, J. Elliott, Smart, and F. Bower; the last-named on April 2 pursued, with his patrol, six hostile scouts a long way east of Douai in a very strong westerly wind, and though shot through the stomach and with his intestines hanging out, he flew west and landed his machine near Chipilly, completely undamaged

except from enemy bullets. He died next day,
and his machine was flown back to the squadron
without having had to be repaired by another
pilot. A fight as a result of which R. B. Clark,
an Australian, was killed on April 30 is well
described below :

"60 Squadron R.F.C.,
"B.E.F., France.
"*April* 1917.

" We are all feeling rather down in our luck
to-day, as news has come through that one of our
chaps has ' gone west ' in hospital. He put up
an awfully ' stout ' show against the Hun.

" It was on one of our big balloon shows. He
was attacked by three Hun scouts just after firing
at the ' gas-bag.' He scrapped them all the way
back to the lines, crashing one of them, and holding
the other two off. As he crossed the trenches,
one of them plugged him in the petrol tank, and
his grid caught on fire. As he was only about
50 feet up, he managed to get her down in the
shell-holes, or rather a strip of ground between
them, without burning himself badly. Luck was
all against him, however, as he just tippled over
into a trench at the end of his run. A few men
who were in an advanced dressing-station near-by
quickly came to his rescue, and hauled him clear
of the burning wreckage, but the poor devil was by
this time badly singed about the legs. He insisted on giving his report before allowing the

doctor to attend to his burns, and the men told me afterwards that he was extremely plucky.

" The day after this occurred, I was detailed to find the machine and see if it could be salved. The weather was absolutely vile. We started for Arras with a tender and trailer,[1] got there about noon, and commenced making inquiries as to where the machine had crashed. One place was pointed out to us where there was an old ' quirk,'[2] which had obviously been brought down doing artillery work. Then we were sent off in another direction, only to find the remains of an old Boche two-seater. At last, after an hour's wading in trenches with mud up to our knees and shells bursting near us, we arrived at the advanced dressing-station. Here we were given a full description of the fine way in which our pilot had fought.

" The machine, needless to say, was a total wreck, and so, after a cup of tea with a drop of gin in it to warm us up, we pushed off home, followed by some heavy shells which we knew meant the commencement of the ' evening hate.' "[3]

Hardly a day passed during April and May without Bishop destroying at least one Hun machine, and on June 2, 1917, he visited an enemy

---

[1] A vehicle used for moving dismantled aeroplanes by road.
[2] A pet name used for artillery machines of the B.E. type.
[3] The Huns always used to bombard certain areas in the morning and evening. These bombardments were known as the morning and evening hate.

aerodrome near Cambrai—a long way over—by himself at dawn and found seven machines on the ground with their engines running. They began to take off and he destroyed four, returning safely with his machine considerably shot about by machine-gun fire from the ground. For this exploit, after three months of remarkably fine work, he was awarded the Victoria Cross. Others who were prominent during the battles of Arras and Vimy Ridge were : Pidcock, " Red " Lloyd and " Black " Lloyd (the latter, a fine officer, was unfortunately shot down and killed), and Fry (who drove down a Hun on our side and found in the pilot's pocket a ticket for a box in Cambrai theatre dated the day before). Molesworth also was doing well ; he afterwards went to 29 on a second tour of duty with the R.F.C. in France (he had already seen service overseas with the infantry), where he did most brilliantly during the winter of 1917–18. His account of a successful balloon attack is given here in full:

> " 60 SQUADRON R.F.C.,
> " B.E.F., FRANCE.
> "*April* 1917.

" Still more excitement ! I tackled my first balloon yesterday, and consider it even more difficult than going for a Hun ; at least, I think one gets a hotter time. We had received orders a week ago that all balloons *had* be to driven down or destroyed, as they were worrying our infantry and gunners during the advance.

" We had been practising firing the Le Prieur rockets [1] for some time—a most weird performance. One dives at a target on the ground, and when within about fifty yards of it presses a button on the instrument board. Immediately there is a most awful hissing noise, which can be heard above the roar of the engine, and six huge rockets shoot forward from the struts each side towards the target.

" We did not think these were much of a success, owing to the difficulty of hitting anything, so decided to use tracer [2] and Buckingham bullets instead. These are filled with a compound of phosphorus and leave a long trail of smoke behind them.

" On the morning we were detailed to attack the balloons the weather was so ' dud ' that none of them were up, although we went across twice to have a look. We got a pretty hot time from Archie, as we had to fly below the clouds, which were about 2,000 feet, and dodge about all over the shop. Next day the weather cleared and we decided to carry out our strafe.

---

[1] These rockets were invented by a Frenchman and used for balloon strafing. They were placed in cases on the struts, and were fired by electricity. The rocket was about $1\frac{1}{2}$ feet long and the stick about 3 feet.

[2] These are used, generally in the ratio of one to four ordinary or armour-piercing bullets, to show the general direction in which the burst of fire is going. Instead of being filled with lead like the ordinary bullet, they contain phosphorus, which commences to burn as soon as the bullet is discharged from the machine gun, and leaves behind it a trail of smoke and fire to mark its course.

" We all went off individually to the various balloons which had been allotted us. I am glad to say most of us managed to do them down. I personally crossed the trenches at about 10,000 feet, dropping all the time towards my sausage, which was five or six miles away. It was floating in company with another at about 3,000 feet, and reminded me of that little song, ' Two Little Sausages.'

" I started a straight dive towards them, and then the fun began. Archie got quite annoyed, following me down to about 5,000 feet, where I was met by two or three strings of flaming onions,[1] luckily too far off to do any damage. Then came thousands of machine-gun bullets from the ground—evidently I was not going to get them without some trouble. I zigzagged about a bit, still heading for the balloons, and when within two hundred yards opened fire. The old Huns in the basket got wind up and jumped out in their parachute. Not bothering about them, I kept my sight on one of the balloons and saw the tracer going right into it and causing it to smoke.

" As our armament consists of a Lewis gun,[2] I had to now change drums. This is a pretty ticklish job when you have about ten machine guns loosing off at you, not to mention all the

[1] A number of balls of fire fastened together and shot up into the air in order to fall over the attacking machine and bring it down in flames.

[2] A type of machine gun. The bullets are fed from a " drum " which is automatically turned when the gun fires.

other small trifles ! However, I managed to do
it without getting more than half a dozen or so
bullet-holes in my grid.

" By this time the second balloon was almost
on the floor. I gave it a burst, which I don't
think did any damage. The first sausage was in
flames, so I buzzed off home without meeting any
Huns. On the way back a good shot from Archie
exploded very near my tail, and carried away part
of the elevator.[1] Don't you think this is the limit
for anyone who wants excitement ? I must say
I prefer it to the infantry, as one gets decent food
and a comfortable bed every night, if you are
lucky enough to get back.

" I am afraid these letters are awfully full of my
own ' shows,' but none of the other chaps will tell
me about theirs, so I can't describe them to you ;
however, it's much the same for all of us. Please
forgive me, and don't think it's swank !

" There are rumours that leave is going to start
again soon, so I hope to see you in a few weeks."

One day in early June General Allenby, then
commanding the 3rd Army, was to inspect the
squadron at nine o'clock in the morning. The
squadron commander had gone out by himself in
his Nieuport at dawn ,unshaved, in pyjamas, a Bur-
berry, bedroom slippers and snowboots, a costume
which many of us used to affect on the dawn

[1] The tail plane which is used to direct the machine up or
down.

patrol. The line was unusually quiet that morning, so he ventured almost to Douai, and on turning west saw a formation of eight or nine machines over Vis-en-Artois, near the front line, well below him at about 8,000 feet. They turned, and the sun glinting on the fuselage showed a bright flash of red. This meant that they were Huns, and not only Huns but " the Circus." Having the advantage of height, and as the formation was very near the line, he determined to try and do a little damage. He flew towards them from the east and from the sun, and diving on the top machine, fired a burst and pulled sharply up, being careful to retain his height. After a few dives of this kind without doing much apparent damage, an S.E.5 patrol of 56, which had seen the scrap, bustled up, and a very pretty " dog-fight " ensued, in the course of which one of the Huns detached himself from the mêlée and appeared to be going home. This was the Nieuport's opportunity, so, hardening his heart, he dived right in, making good shooting. The Albatros appeared to take no notice, but flew straight on. (In parenthesis it may be observed that this is a good sign, as it usually means the pilot is dead, for if the opposing machine begins to perform frantic evolutions, the pilot is as a rule very much alive, and not in the least " out of control.") Flushed with excitement, the Nieuport man put the stick (control column) between his knees, and going down on the tail of the Albatros, began

to put a fresh drum of ammunition on to his
Lewis gun, with which alone this type of machine
was armed. While thus busily engaged something made him turn his head to see about twenty
yards behind him the white nose of a grim-looking
Albatros. Swifter than thought the Nieuport was
wrenched to the right, and even as she turned the
Albatros's Spandau guns spat out a burst, which
riddled the engine and cut the bottom out of the
petrol tank, allowing all the remaining petrol to
pour on to the pilot's feet. The height of both
machines at this moment was about 5,000 feet,
the locality just east of Monchy-le-Preux, and but
for the attentions of the Boche machine it would
have been comparatively easy for the Nieuport to
glide back to Arras and perch on one of our advanced landing-grounds, or on the race-course;
but with a bloodthirsty Hun on one's tail and a
dead engine, the problem, however, was not such
a simple one. Twisting and turning like a snipe,
the Nieuport began to descend, taking care to
make his turns as much as possible towards our
side of the line. Mercifully the wind was from
the east. Close behind followed the Albatros,
firing short bursts at frequent intervals, but
always wide, because it is not easy to hit a machine
whose pilot knows you are there. It was a stout
Hun, however, who would not be denied, but continued the chase down to 300 feet, a few hundred
yards west of Monchy-le-Preux, when he suddenly
turned and flew home to report, no doubt, a

British machine destroyed. With a gasp of relief the Nieuport pilot turned his attention to the ground, and, seeing nothing but shell-holes beneath him, made up his mind that a crash was inevitable. Suddenly a strip of ground about a hundred yards long and very narrow, but free from shell-holes, caught his eye, and, putting in a couple of "S" turns, he made a good slow landing. The machine ran on and had almost stopped when a shell-hole appeared, and she ran very gently into it without doing any damage whatever.

A couple of dusty gunners walked up and before speaking produced a packet of Woodbines, one of which the Nieuport pilot greedily took and lit. Inquiries showed that an advanced anti-aircraft section was near-by, where the officer-in-charge gave the airman breakfast and, better still, produced a telephone, with the help of which he got into communication with his squadron, and ordered a car to come straight through Arras and up the Cambrai road. It was getting late, and an Army Commander's inspection was not a thing to be treated lightly. Further inquiries disclosed an Artillery Ammunition Column in a little valley who lent him a horse and an orderly. There was no saddle, but the pilot climbed grate-fully on to the animal, which had very rough paces and a hard mouth, and set out towards the road. In a short time he met the car and drove furiously through Arras and back to Le Hameau, only to see Allenby, the R.F.C. Brigade Commander (General J. R. Higgins), and George Pretyman arriving at the station. His costume being hardly that prescribed for inspections, the wretched officer dived into his hut, did the quickest shave on record, and timidly approached the glittering cortège.

Everyone was furious with him except General Allenby, who was rather amused and very kind. He got, however, a well-deserved and proper " telling-off" from the Brigadier and Wing Commander, and saw the troupe depart with a feeling of profound relief.

The account of this scrap has been given at some length, but it should not be assumed that it was in any way exceptional. It should be remembered that during the squadron's history there have been about 1,500 distinct combats in the air, all of which deserve a detailed description. Within the limits of a book of this kind, however, it cannot be done.

We made a hard tennis-court in Tetus's orchard with red *pierre de fosse* from the Bruay mines, and discovered that Caldwell, Molesworth, Horn, and both Lloyds were all good tennis players. With the beginning of June things quietened down on the 3rd Army front. Colonel Pretyman, O.C. 13th Wing, put the squadron on to wireless interception. This term needs, perhaps, a little explanation. Everyone knows, of course, that both German and British artillery observation machines were fitted with wireless sets, by means of which the pilots corrected the shooting of the gunners for whom they were observing.

These wireless messages were " tapped " by our compass stations, and it was discovered that two of these stations could get a cross-bearing on any machines registering for the enemy artillery. By linking up the compass station with an aerodrome by telephone, it was possible to send off a patrol of scouts to chase off or destroy the artillery machine as soon as he began to send down fire signals, i.e. as soon as he was actually directing the fire of the enemy batteries. This was useful, though exhausting work for pilots ; for the Hun, who did his registration chiefly in the morning, when the sun was behind him in the east, usually saw the scouts coming before they saw him, and turned and dived three or four miles back behind his own lines, where it was very difficult to attack him, even if he was visible, which usually he was not, as our scouts were looking for a machine at five or six thousand feet in a certain place, whereas it was probably at that moment at a height of 1,500 feet some five miles east of the bearing given. As soon, therefore, as the scouts, seeing nothing, turned back to return to the aerodrome, the Hun swung up again and resumed his registration. The British pilots, on returning to their aerodrome, would find an irate squadron commander who had just got a telephone message from the compass station to say that V.K., or whatever the call sign used by that particular machine might be, was working again quite happily, and, "What the devil was 60's patrol doing, anyhow?" Off the wretched patrol had to go again, only to go through the same performance. It is only fair to say, however, that they did get a good many two-seaters in this way, though the main result was, perhaps, seen rather in the enormously decreased amount of artillery observation the Germans were enabled to do, than in hostile artillery machines shot down by us.

This work, however, was genuinely exhausting, as in order efficiently to answer the compass calls, as they were termed, three or four pilots always had to be standing by to leap into their machines and be off the ground, in formation, inside of two minutes. Nevertheless, they became extraordinarily smart at this manœuvre, and answered to the hunting horn—doubled blasts of which were the signal at that time—as keenly as a fashionable pack of foxhounds. Only those who know how irritating a thing an aero engine can be when you are in a hurry to start can appreciate the high standard of efficiency attained by 60's mechanics, which made it almost a certainty that the 120 seconds limit would not be exceeded.

The next few paragraphs will show how this manœuvre struck one of the pilots at this time :

"60 Squadron R.F.C.,
"B.E.F., France.
"*July* 1917.

" The tennis-court we made three months ago is now in topping condition, so we decided to get up a tournament amongst ourselves. Yesterday we drew lots for partners. The unlucky lad who drew me is a ' coloured troop,' that is he hails from South Africa. He is quite good at the ' Willies,' [1] and so I think we have got a fair chance. I expect you wonder where all these weird names come from. They are invented by one of our flight commanders, who is also a ' coloured troop ' and one of the leading lights of the squadron. All jobs are washed out to-day as the weather is ' dud,' so two of us are going over this afternoon to the village near-by to purchase articles of furniture for the ' Hôtel de Commerce.'

" You will be pleased to hear that we are getting a new kind of grid. It is supposed to be a good deal faster than the Hun, and can dive to 300 miles an hour, so I'm told. We shall probably have a quiet time while we are getting used to them, and only do ' line patrols ' for the first fortnight or so. A French ' Ace ' [2] landed here to-day ; he says the Huns are getting a pretty bad time down south. Jolly glad I'm not a Hun airman these days, with men up against me like some of our chaps. Most of them are fairly old

---

[1] Tennis.

[2] A pilot who has brought down five or more enemy machines.

hands at the game now, and we are really beginning to properly annoy our friends across the way.
The work has been fairly hard lately : two patrols
in the morning, one generally at dawn and the
other about noon, with ' wireless interruption ' in
the afternoon. The latter is rather a strenuous
job. This is how we work it : When a Hun
two-seater begins to register on any part of our
front, a telephone message, giving his height and
locality, is immediately sent through to the wireless squadron. Each scout squadron in the wing
takes it in turn. As soon as the Recording Officer[1]
receives the message, he sounds a horn. Three of
us who are standing by in readiness immediately
jump into our machines, and the leader gets hold
of the position and height of the Hun. Then we
push off as quickly as possible to the lines, and a
sort of ' hide-and-seek ' begins. We try if possible
to hide in the clouds and approach the Hun when
he is off his guard. He, on the other hand,
departs hurriedly into Hunland when he spots us,
and as soon as we go he comes back to carry on his
job. We then turn on him again, but he is off
like a flash, and so it goes on until the next three
machines relieve us. It is really quite amusing
at times, and, although we do not often bring our
man down, we give him such a devil of a time that
he hasn't much of it to spare for his companions
on the ground. Our ' stunt merchant '[2] is good

---

[1] Corresponds to an Adjutant in an infantry battalion.
[2] Bishop.

at this game, and continues to add to his score, seldom coming back without firing his red light. He works by himself a lot now, preferring to surprise the Hun by hiding rather than by trying to get him in a scrap. Wish I could do the same. I always feel so fagged after a patrol, that I haven't got the energy or the patience to sit up in the clouds waiting for a chance to bag a ' lone Hun.'

" You remember the petrol tank which was so shot up the time I was brought down ? Well, I am having it made into a topping inkstand. The souvenirs are coming in in fine style, and I hope to have quite a good collection by the time I see dear old ' Blighty ' again."

After the battle had died down the sorely tried pilots were given, whenever possible, one day's rest in three, and the following letter shows that the device was appreciated :

" 60 SQUADRON R.F.C.,
" B.E.F., FRANCE.
" *June* 1917.

" It is funny hearing the war again after being on leave so long. We had quite a good crossing, although I had a deuce of a time getting on to the boat at Folkestone. The silly ass of a porter had carted all my baggage on board, including the leave warrant, which was in my British-warm pocket. I had to persuade the A.M.L.O.[1] I wasn't

---

[1] *A.M.L.O. :* Assistant Military Landing Officer.

a Hun spy, and, after a long discussion, he let me on.

" The Major seemed pleased to have me back, and they all had great stories to tell about our ' stunt merchant,'[1] who had been putting up a jolly good show by bringing down umpteen[2] Huns. His star turn was the shooting up of an aerodrome. He started off at dawn by himself and arrived over the aerodrome he had planned to attack. Finding that there was nothing doing here, he pushed off to look for trouble elsewhere. Suddenly he saw the hangars of another aerodrome. He attacked these with much gusto, and when the Huns came up to do him down, he crashed two of them and drove another into the trees. He also managed to flatten out a large number of mechanics and put pukka wind up the rest. You can imagine how the fat old Huns ran, as nothing like this had ever happened to them before. I believe his name has been put in for something big in the decoration line.

" It has been arranged that we get one day off in every three, which gives us a bit of spare time. We had ours off to-day. Four of us aviated over to Paris-Plage, near Etaples, this afternoon and tested our grids by firing into the sea. Afterwards we landed opposite the Hôtel Continental and left our machines there under a guard. We wandered about the village for a bit, and then

[1] Bishop, who got his V.C. for this.

[2] An indefinitely large number.

started for home, stunting [1] about to amuse the populace, which had collected on the front to see us off. We all got home safely just as it was getting dark."

[1] Trick flying.

BALLOON STRAFING.
Attacking an enemy kite balloon with incendiary ammunition.
By Capt. W. E. Molesworth, M.C.

PATROL OF MORANE "BULLETS" ABOUT TO LEAVE THE GROUND, VERT GALANT, JUNE 1916.

H. BALFOUR AND D. V. ARMSTRONG, JULY 1916.

CLAUDE A. RIDLEY, M.C., IN A MORANE "BULLET"

MAJOR R. SMITH-BARRY IN A MORANE "BULLET."

SUMMERS STANDING BY HIS MORANE "PARASOL."

CAPT. D. V. ARMSTRONG.

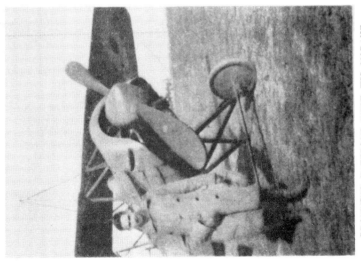

BROWNING PATERSON WITH HIS MORANE "PARASOL."

SOME OF THE OFFICERS OF 60.
Front row: Bell Irving, Reid, and Meintjies.

MORANE "BULLET" CRASHED BY SIMPSON. BOISDINGHEM, JUNE 1916.

"A" FLIGHT AWAITING SIGNAL TO PROCEED ON PATROL, MAY 1917.

THE KAISER DECORATING VON RICHTHOFEN, WHOSE AEROPLANE
APPEARS BEYOND THE GROUP.

Hindenburg and the German Crown Prince figure in the group on the left.

BISHOP, CALDWELL, AND YOUNG, APRIL 1917.

MOLESWORTH, BISHOP, AND CALDWELL, APRIL 1917.

THE HARD TENNIS-COURT AT FILESCAMP FARM, MAY 1917.

60 SQUADRON'S NIEUPORT SCOUTS LINED UP IN THE SNOW AT
FILESCAMP FARM, JANUARY 1917

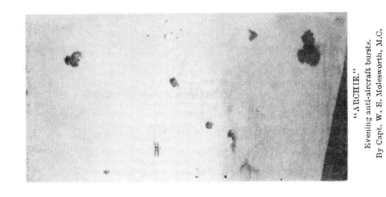

A DOG-FIGHT.
Nieuports v. Albatros.
By Capt. W. E. Molesworth, M.C.

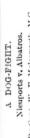

"ARCHIE."
Evening anti-aircraft bursts.
By Capt. W. E. Molesworth, M.C.

GERMAN MACHINES.
The largest is a DHI Albatros.
By Capt. W. E. Molesworth, M.C.

AN S.E.A. WITH LIEUT. ROTH, A PILOT OF 148 AMERICAN SQUADRON, STANDING.

S.E.5A, WITH 200 H.P. HISPANO SUISA ENGINE, ARMED WITH ONE VICKERS AND ONE LEWIS GUN.

CHAPTER IV

THE centre of interest had now (June 1917) shifted to the North. The Messines Ridge had been taken, though we heard nothing of it till it was over, and many of the Hun *Jagdstaffeln*, as their scout squadrons were called, had moved up to Flanders.

On July 22, Scott, who had been wounded in the arm a few days before, was promoted wing commander and sent to the XI or Army Wing of the 2nd Brigade allotted to the 2nd Army in the Ypres sector. C. K. Cochrane-Patrick, D.S.O., M.C., who had been doing brilliantly in 23 Squadron on Spads, succeeded to the command of 60, who were at that time being re-equipped with 150 h.p. S.E.5s, this being the newest type of scouts, as the Nieuports were by then rather out of date.

Not quite so much fighting was done during July and August, as the change of machines from an air-cooled rotary engine (the 110 h.p. Le Rhone which had served us so well) to a 150 h.p. water-cooled stationary (the Hispano Suisa) naturally took some getting used to. These machines were

5

again replaced in late August with 200 h.p. Hispano
Suisa S.E.5s, which, though a more powerful engine
than the 150 h.p., was much more difficult to
keep serviceable.   Nevertheless, Bishop (who was
soon posted to Home Establishment—H.E., as the
R.F.C. called it), Caldwell, Rutherford, W. Jenkins (afterwards killed in a collision with West-
Thompson over Poperinghe), Molesworth, M.C.
and bar, Hall, S. B. Horn, M.C. (whose dog Lobo
was a squadron pet), and G. Lloyd, M.C. (who was
promoted to captain and sent to 40 Squadron as
flight commander), were all distinguishing themselves and adding to the squadron's laurels.

In the following extract Molesworth again
graphically describes a fight in which he was very
nearly killed :

"60 SQUADRON R.F.C.,
"B.E.F., FRANCE.
"*June* 1917.

" Yesterday I had the narrowest shave I've
ever had since I first started Boche-strafing.   I
was properly caught out this time, and really
thought things were all up.

" We were just over the Drocourt Switch,[1] near
Vitry, when a dozen Huns got what you might call
' uppish.'   We tumbled into a proper mix-up and,
as there were only five of us, the Huns managed
to break up our formation.   We had arranged
that, should this happen, we were to return to the

---

[1] A formidable line of trenches branching off from the main
Hindenburg line of Queant and defending Douai.

line independently and re-form, so I started towards Arras, following the Scarpe.[1]

" Just as I was passing over Gavrelle I espied three fat Hun two-seaters making south-east.

" ' Here we are, my son,' says I to myself. ' We'll just hop down and put the gust [2] up one of these Huns.'

" No sooner said than done. I pushed my nose down and, when within range, opened fire. The next thing I knew was a perfect hail of bullets pouring round me. Here is a rough description of my thoughts during the few minutes that followed :

" Crackle ! crackle ! crackle !

" ' My cheery aunt ! There's a Hun on my tail.'

" ' By jove ! The blighter is making my grid into a sieve. Confound him ! '

" ' Let's pull her up in a good climbing turn and have a look at him.'

" ' Heavens ! It's "the Circus." '[3]

" ' I wonder if old Richthof is the leader. The dirty dog nearly caught me out this time. Silly ass ! didn't hold his fire long enough, or he'd have made me into cold meat by now.'

" ' Let's give him a dose and see how he likes it.'

---

[1] A stream flowing north of Arras.

[2] Same as wind up, or fright.

[3] One of the most famous formations of enemy scouts, composed of the " crack " German pilots. Their machines generally had red bodies.

" ' Here he comes straight at me, loosing off with both guns.'

" ' I hope we aren't going to collide.'

" ' Missed ! Bon ! Everything's **A1.** Wish I'd hit him, though ! '

" ' I must pull her round quick or he will be on my tail.'

" ' Hang ! I can't shoot for toffee, but he's pretty " dud," too, thank heavens ! '

" ' Once again, boys, round with her. Let him have it hot.'

" ' No good. Try again.'

" ' Confound it ! There's my beastly drum empty. I must spin and change it.'

" ' Good enough ! Now where's the blighter ? '

" ' My Harry ! He has got me stiff this time ; here he comes down on me from the right.'

" Crack ! crack ! crack ! bang ! zip ! zip !

" ' There goes my petrol tank ; now for the flames.'

" ' Cheero ! No luck this time, you old swine. Wait till I get you next show.'

" ' Here goes for the ground.'

" Luckily for me, my friend and his pals, who had been watching the scrap, thought I was done for. They therefore chucked up the sponge and departed.

" I managed to pull the machine out, just scraping over the trenches. The engine was still running, although the petrol was pouring out all over my legs. A few minutes afterwards the engine conked out altogether, and I had to land in a field. I was immediately surrounded by a crowd of men, who had seen the fight. Amongst them were some artillery officers, who took me off to their mess and offered me a ' tot,' which was very thankfully received, while they sent off a message to the squadron. The following is the official list of damage done to my machine :

" Six bullet holes in propeller.

" Cowling [1] shot away.

" Large holes in bottom of petrol tank and sides.

" Main spar [2] right-hand top plane broken.

" Rear right-hand under-carriage strut badly damaged.

" Twenty-eight holes in fuselage [3] and ten in the planes—two or three missing the pilot's seat by less than an inch."

During the 3rd Corps' attack on August 19, 1917, Lieuts. Jenkins, Steele, Thompson, Rutherford, and Sergt. Bancroft did good work shooting up infantry in trenches and by harassing the troops assembling for counter-attacks.

On September 7, 1917, the squadron was moved up to the XI Wing to help in the battles for the Passchendale Ridge, which were already in full swing. Leaving the comfortable Filescamp station and the hard tennis-court with great regret,

[1] A piece of aluminium shaped so as to cover the engine.

[2] A main plane is made up of two spars on which the ribs are fixed.

[3] Body of the machine.

they were moved into tents on Marie Capelle aerodrome, near Cassel, where 20 Squadron was already stationed. The 2nd and 5th Armies were then attacking almost every day, and 60, in addition to their ordinary work of offensive patrols, wireless interception, etc., co-operated by low flying and firing at troops and transport on the ground. Twenty-five-pound Cooper bombs were carried at this time and dropped on suitable targets.

Capt. Chidlaw-Roberts, Lieuts. Rutherford, Whiting, and I. Macgregor were now prominent, while Patrick, himself a brilliant fighter, was always ready to give his squadron a lead.

Chidlaw-Roberts got a lot of Huns during September, and Caldwell and W. Jenkins continued their successes of the summer, while J. Crompton, Young, Capt. Hammersley, Lieut. W. Sherwood, and 2/Lieut. Carter were others who were conspicuous during the October fighting.

It was in September that Capt. J. K. Law, one of the sons of Mr. Bonar Law (another of whose sons had already been killed in Mesopotamia), joined at Marie Capelle. He was a tiger to fight, and, had he come through his first month, would probably have made a great name for himself. He did several " shows " over the line, and his machine was shot about badly in every one of them. On September 21, a patrol operating in the neighbourhood of Roulers, led by Hammersley and including Whiting and Macgregor and Law, saw twenty-four hostile machines and engaged eight of them. A general engagement took place, in the course of which Law was shot down and killed. He had absolutely refused to stay any longer at home, where he was doing most useful work training pilots, but insisted on being sent to France.

Life was less easy during the autumn, as the Boche had begun continually to send over night-bombing machines. Our scouts were not very successful in dealing with them, for it is very difficult to see another machine in the air at night even though it may be visible from the ground; and, although several attempts were made at this time by 70 and 29 Squadrons, stationed at Poperinghe, to attack these night bombers, they never succeeded in engaging one. The chief difficulty was that one could not ask pilots and mechanics to work all night as well as all day. If it had been possible to take a scout squadron or two off day work and set them to deal only with the German night bombers, there is little doubt but that they would have achieved some measure of success in spite of the shortage of searchlights. The authorities, however, would not hear of this, as there was too much to be done by day to spare one of our none too numerous fighter squadrons for night work. Much later in the war, July 1918 to be exact, 151 Squadron was sent out equipped with Camels fitted for night flying, and this squadron alone very nearly exterminated the

Boche night bombers on the 1st and 3rd Army fronts. It was in this squadron that D. V. Armstrong added so greatly to the reputation he had already gained, and it was with them that he was killed. As things were, however, in 1917 the enemy dropped their bombs nightly almost with impunity, as anti-aircraft fire was not very effective at night, and machine-gun fire from the ground was useless against machines which rarely flew lower than 5,000 feet.

During this autumn series of battles a somewhat novel system of message-dropping was tried. All scout pilots were ordered to carry cards conveniently fixed in the nacelle, on which they wrote such information as they had secured during low-flying patrols ; special attention was to be given to the massing of enemy supporting troops and to the development of counter-attacks, the symptoms of which were the approach to the " debussing " [1] points of motor transport vehicles or trains from which troops could be seen disembarking and forming up. These cards were slipped into a message bag and dropped in a field marked with a white cross, near Locre Château, not far from the line, which was the 2nd Army report centre. The information thus given occasionally enabled our heavy artillery to direct their fire on to the targets indicated. On one occasion, in October, a pilot reported a big gun being

[1] A barbarous word invented by the Army, and which means " alighting from an omnibus."

moved along a road near Menin; the Corps heavies opened on it within ten minutes of the message being dropped, and another pilot of another squadron reported, half an hour later, a heavy gun at the same place to have been destroyed by a direct hit. Information of this kind was very necessary, as the German policy at that time was to hold their front line positions lightly against our initial assaults, but to counter-attack very strongly and swiftly about two hours or so after our first attack had been delivered.

Lieuts. F. Soden, W. Rutherford, and W. Duncan all distinguished themselves by giving accurate information during these battles, while Selous, a son of the big-game hunter, was also proving himself to be a fine patrol leader and Hun-getter.

The last-named—the worthy son of a famous father—was killed on January 4, 1918, while leading his patrol. He dived at some enemy machines several thousand feet below, and in the middle of his dive, the speed of which the other members of the patrol estimated at not less than 300 miles per hour, the wings of his S.E.5 came right off.

As good a flight commander as ever we had, he was a very great loss to the squadron. Without, perhaps, the brilliance of Ball or Bishop he, like Caldwell, Summers, Armstrong, Hammersley, Chidlaw-Roberts, Belgrave, and Scholte, to name a few only of the best, played always for the squadron, and not for his own hand. He took endless pains to enter young pilots to the game, watching them on their first patrols as a good and patient huntsman watches his young hounds.

The character of Selous, like those whom I have mentioned, not to speak of many others whom their comrades will remember, attained very nearly to the ideal of a gentleman's character as described by Burke, Newman, and Cavendish in the extracts given below, for which I am indebted to a report by Lord Hugh Cecil on the education of the future R.A.F. officer. These noble sentiments so fully describe the kind of man the British love and admire that it is perhaps not inappropriate to quote them :

" Character of a Gentleman

" But the age of chivalry is gone. That of sophisters, economists, and calculators has succeeded ; and the glory of Europe is extinguished for ever. Never, never more shall we behold that generous loyalty to rank and sex, that proud submission, that dignified obedience, that subordination of the heart, which kept alive, even in servitude itself, the spirit of an exalted freedom. The unbought grace of life, the cheap defence of nations, the nurse of manly sentiment and heroic enterprise is gone ! It is gone, that sensibility of principle, that chastity of honour, which felt a stain like a wound, which inspired courage whilst it mitigated ferocity, which ennobled whatever it touched, and under which vice itself lost half its evil, by losing all its grossness.

" This mixed system of opinion and sentiment had its origin in the ancient chivalry ; and the principle, though varied in its appearance by the varying state of human affairs, subsisted and influenced through a long succession of generations, even to the time we live in. If it should ever be totally extinguished, the loss, I fear, will be great. It is this which has given its character to modern Europe. It is this which has distinguished it under all its forms of government, and distinguished it to its advantage, from the states of Asia, and possibly from those states which flourished in the most brilliant periods of the antique world. It was this which, without confounding ranks, had produced a noble equality, and handed it down through all the gradations of social life. It was this opinion which mitigated kings into companions, and raised private men to be fellows with kings. Without force or opposition, it subdued the fierceness of pride and power ; it obliged sovereigns to submit to the soft collar of social esteem, compelled stern authority to submit to elegance, and gave a dominating vanquisher of laws to be subdued by manners."

(BURKE : *Reflections on the Revolution in France.*)

" Hence it is that it is almost a definition of a gentleman to say that he is one who never inflicts pain. This description is both refined and, as far as it goes, accurate. He is mainly occupied in merely removing the obstacles which hinder the free and unembarrassed action of those about him ; and he concurs with their movements rather than takes the initiative himself. His benefits may be considered as parallel to what are called comforts or conveniences in arrangements of a personal nature : like an easy-chair or a good fire, which do their part in dispelling cold and fatigue, though nature provides both means of rest and animal heat without them. The true gentleman in like manner carefully avoids whatever may cause a jar or a jolt in the minds of those with whom he is cast—all clashing of opinion or collision of feeling, all restraint or suspicion, or gloom, or resentment; his great concern being to make everyone at their ease and at home. He has his eyes on all his company ; he is tender towards the bashful, gentle towards the distant, and merciful towards the absurd ; he can recollect to whom he is speaking ; he guards against unseasonable allusions, or topics which may irritate ; he is seldom prominent in conversation and never wearisome. He makes light of favours when he does them, and seems to be receiving when he is conferring. He never speaks of himself except when compelled, never defends himself by a mere retort ; he has no ears for

slander or gossip, is scrupulous in imputing
motives to those who interfere with him, and
interprets everything for the best. He is never
mean or little in his disputes, never takes unfair
advantage, never mistakes personalities or sharp
sayings for arguments, or insinuates evil which he
dare not say out. From a long-sighted prudence
he observes the maxim of the ancient sage, that
we should ever conduct ourselves towards our
enemy as if he were one day to be our friend.
He has too much good sense to be affronted at
insults, he is too well employed to remember
injuries, and too indolent to bear malice. He is
patient, forbearing, and resigned, on philosophical
principles; he submits to pain, because it is
inevitable, to bereavement, because it is irrepar-
able, and to death, because it is his destiny. If
he engages in controversy of any kind, his dis-
ciplined intellect preserves him from the blunder-
ing discourtesy of better, perhaps, but less
educated minds; who, like blunt weapons, tear
and hack instead of cutting clean, who mistake
the point in argument, waste their strength on
trifles, misconceive their adversary, and leave
the question more involved than they find it.
He may be right or wrong in his opinion, but he
is too clear-headed to be unjust; he is as simple
as he is forcible, and as brief as he is decisive.
Nowhere shall we find greater candour, consideration, indulgence: he throws himself into the
minds of his opponents, he accounts for their

mistakes. He knows the weakness of human reason as well as its strength, its province, and its limits. If he be an unbeliever, he will be too profound and large-minded to ridicule religion or to act against it ; he is too wise to be a dogmatist or fanatic in his infidelity. He respects piety and devotion ; he even supports institutions as venerable, beautiful, or useful, to which he does not assent ; he honours the ministers of religion, and it contents him to decline its mysteries without assailing or denouncing them. He is a friend of religious toleration, and that, not only because his philosophy has taught him to look on all forms of faith with an impartial eye, but also from the gentleness and effeminacy of feeling which is the attendant on civilisation."

(NEWMAN : *Idea of a University*, Discourse VIII, Section 10.)

" He has besides the principle of common honesty, which would prevent him from doing wrong, a principle of nice honour, which will always urge him to do right. By honour I do not mean a fashionable mistaken principle which would only lead a man to court popular reputation and avoid popular disgrace, whether the opinion upon which they are founded is false or true ; whether the conduct which they require is in itself just or unjust, or its consequences hurtful or beneficial to mankind. I mean a quality which is not satisfied with doing right when it is merely

the alternative of wrong ; which prompts a man
to do what he might lawfully and honestly leave
undone ; which distinguishes a thousand different
shades in what is generally denominated the same
colour, and is as much superior to a mere con-
formity to prescribed rules as forgiving a debt is
to paying what we owe."

(LORD JOHN CAVENDISH : From speech pro-
posing Mr. Thos. Tounshend for Speaker,
1770. *Parliamentary History*, vol. xvi, col.
737, A.D. 1770.)

On November 8, Pope, an old member of the
squadron, who had come through the Arras battle
with us, destroyed two hostile two-seaters in one
day. This was a good pilot and a popular officer,
who for some reason was a long time before he
began to get Huns, but, having once found his
form, became a very useful and formidable
fighter. He went home soon after this, and
showed himself to be an exceptionally gifted
trainer of pilots, both in flying and fighting.

On November 20 the Cambrai attack was
launched by the 1st and 3rd Armies, and the
pressure in the air on the Passchendale sector
became sensibly less. This meant that the low-
flying patrols, which were extra to the ordinary
O.P. work, ceased for the time being, a relief
which was very welcome because low flying was
never popular, the pilot being not only exposed
to very severe fire from the ground, but also,

being so low, was at a disadvantage when meeting enemy machines, who could dive upon him at their leisure, and frequently availed themselves of this privilege.

By this time they had made themselves quite comfortable at Marie Capelle, and the necessary precautions had been taken to give protection against bombs. It is really remarkable how soon a good squadron will make itself at home in a new station, and how, if all ranks work together, messes, recreation rooms, and a theatre rise up like pumpkins. Sixty could always make themselves comfortable, as the following extracts from the letters of 2/Lieut. R. W. Maclennan will show. These letters have been collected and published, after Maclennan's death from wounds on December 23, 1917, by his father, a well-known Toronto barrister, who has courteously allowed them to be reprinted. They describe his arrival at the squadron from the base :

"60 Squadron R.F.C.,
"B.E.F., France.
"*November* 28, 1917.

"When the tender came we collected our kit and started on a long cold ride to the aerodrome, which we reached in three-quarters of an hour. The first thing was to report to the squadron commander, a captain who last summer had been one of my instructors. He was in temporary command in the absence of the Major, who was on leave, but has since returned. When we went to the mess we ran into a lot more of Central Flying School boys, who had been there in our time. There are about twenty-four officers in the squadron, and more than half of these are Canadians, so I feel quite at home. As a new-comer I shall not get much flying during the first fortnight. I shall do all I can round the aerodrome for practice, so that when the time comes for me to go over the line I shall know something about it.

" Of all the S.E.5 squadrons in France, we seem to have struck the best. It is one which has done exceedingly well in the past. Both the late Captain Ball and Major Bishop belonged to it, and there have been fewer casualties than in any other similar squadron.[1] Having had so few, the chaps have been in the game a long time, and so have had wide experience, and this is bound to be of inestimable benefit to new people. The aerodrome is a good twenty miles behind the line, and is practically immune from shell fire. None have landed anywhere near for months.

" You ought to see our quarters. I share a hut with three others and we have lots of room. The huts are like half a barrel laid on the ground ; the curved roof is corrugated iron and the ends are wood. We have several tables, comfortable chairs, our camp beds, and innumerable rugs on the floor. A coal stove and an oil stove give

[1] This, I am afraid, is not quite accurate, as a glance at Appendix II will show.

6

plenty of heat, and petrol lamps give excellent light. I have not had such comfortable permanent quarters since leaving Canada, and yet we are within sound range of the guns, which never cease. I was able to bring over practically every article of kit I possessed. An infantry officer would have had to leave nine-tenths of it behind.

"One great comfort is that here we can wear just exactly what we like. We can come to breakfast in pyjamas and wear comfortable old clothes all day long. Puttees I am discarding for good, and in their place will wear long stockings. They have always been an abomination, as their tightness stops circulation and induces cold. We do not wear belts and can fly in sweaters. In fact, it will be a long summer holiday with lots of excitement thrown in. Leave comes round every three months, and lasts for fourteen days."

"60 SQUADRON R.F.C.,
"B.E.F., FRANCE.
"*December* 2, 1917.

"To add to the comfort of the mess, besides dogs, we have a fairly good piano and a gramophone. Every time anyone goes on leave he brings back a few records, and the collection is now quite large.

"The hours for actual flying are of necessity short on account of the shortness of daylight. Consequently we get lots of time for exercise, most of which consists in kicking a Rugby ball around the aerodrome. It is about the best way of keeping warm in these cold days.

" Our tenders frequently run to St. Omer and even as far as Boulogne, so when not flying there are chances of seeing these places. It does seem funny to be able to go from practically the trenches to Boulogne (within sight of England) almost any time we want to. We in the R.F.C. are about the only people who can do this.

" When artillery horses are in need of rest, they are sent back from the front line. We have two or three at the squadron, and I shall probably get some riding if I can pluck up courage enough to try.

" It is bound to be muddy here before the winter is over ; at present everything is dry. In preparation for later we have ' duck-boards,' or wooden slat-walks, laid down between all the huts, the mess, the hangars, etc. On a dark night it is rather a problem to keep on these boards. This reminds me that my little pocket flash lamp is almost indispensable out here.

" All the heavy labour in this part of France is now being done by Chinese coolies, brought specially from China for this purpose. They are enlisted as soldiers and wear a peculiar blue padded uniform. They are employed around the aerodrome levelling ground, putting sand-bags about the huts as a protection against bombs, making roads and paths, etc. They are terribly interested in our phonograph, and if we leave the

door open they almost come in. To keep them
out, the interpreter has painted a large sign in
Chinese characters, and it sticks up in front of the
mess and gives it quite an Oriental appearance.

" Moving picture shows are given every night
or so in a Church Army hut in the camp. We had
several good films last night. It hardly seems at
all like war yet."

" FRANCE,
" *December* 3, 1917.

" I am still merely watching operations from
the ground. Two fresh pilots have been posted
to the squadron since Hemsworth and I arrived,
and we shall probably commence flying to-morrow
if the weather is suitable.

" Great interest is being shown out here in the
coming general election in Canada, and the
authorities are endeavouring to have every
Canadian register his vote. Quite contrary to
army precedent and regulations, the authorities
are openly urging everyone to vote against
Laurier. Most of us share this view, but it is
interesting to see the officials of an army in the
field canvassing votes for one party.

" The Canadians are no longer near us. I
imagine they needed a rest badly after their recent
push.

" You ought to see our strength in dogs. The
squadron boasts sixteen canines at present. The
officers' mess possesses five. We are very proud
of them. Besides these, we have six pigs and

twenty-five hens.   There is no shortage of eggs
about the mess."

"FRANCE,
"December 9, 1917.

" Since last Sunday I have been waiting,
waiting, waiting for a flight, and not till last
Thursday did I get it.   The day was cloudy and
the visibility poor.   Hemsworth and I were to
have a practice flight, and we spent about twenty
minutes at it.   When we finished, I had lost sight
of the aerodrome and so had he, for I could see
him flying aimlessly one way and then another,
diving on one hill and then on several more.   As
our aerodrome is near a town perched on a high
hill, I knew what he was looking for, but none of
the hills seemed to be the right one.   After that
he flew east for a time, and, although I knew such
a course would take us into Hunland, I followed,
deciding to go with him as far as the trenches and
then turn west again.   Just our side of the line I
spotted a town [1] which I recognised from the great
relief map we had at Oxford.   It is a town that
has undergone more shelling than any other during
the whole war.   I never saw such a sight of
desolation.   Nothing but shell-holes in all directions.   Practically all the buildings in ruins, and
every now and then a shell would burst in the
desolate city with a blinding flash.   Of course, I
could hear nothing of the explosion.   I knew my
way back to the aerodrome and felt much relieved,

[1] Ypres.

as it is most undignified to get lost on one's first flip. I opened my engine and soon caught up the other machine, and signalled Hemsworth to turn round and follow me. We were at the aerodrome twenty minutes later. I have not been in the air since owing to a temporary shortage of machines.

". . . The little town [1] near our aerodrome, perched on a high hill, has a fine square, from which a beautiful church can be seen, and the square and streets are cobbled. The road which leads into the town from the east enters through a short tunnel, which emerges right into the square itself. When I was last there, several howitzer batteries were coming from the line for a rest, and the caterpillar tractors, which haul these huge guns, were grunting and chugging from the tunnel into the town, and through it, making for some spot further to the rear. All units which come out of the trenches for a rest are sent far enough back to be out of earshot of the guns. The Casino, at the highest part of the town, is devoted to military purposes. From it a wonderful view of the Western Front may be had, puffs of smoke in the distance, captive sausage observation balloons, aeroplanes, and roads teeming with hundreds and hundreds of motor-lorries slowly crawling along. A batch of miserable-looking German prisoners were engaged in cleaning the streets. Their appearance gave the impression that they must

[1] Cassel.

have been reduced to sorry straits before their capture, as they all looked white, pinched, and sickly. I think they are pretty fairly treated by our people, and certainly given enough to eat.

" Speaking of food reminds me that you may be interested to know that we do pretty well in our mess. I quote from our ordinary dinner menu : Soup (mock turtle), toast; fish (grilled sole, mustard sauce); entrée (beefsteak, pastry, boiled potatoes, green peas); sweets (stewed prunes, cornstarch pudding); biscuits, cheese, coffee. Does this satisfy you ? It does me.

" We have the correct number of machines, six in each flight, and there are three flights, ' A,' ' B,' and ' C.' I am in ' B ' Flight. There are eighteen pilots, an equipment officer who is also quartermaster, a recording officer (adjutant) and the commanding officer. So we have twenty-two in our mess.

" Lunch is served at one o'clock. Sometimes I have spent the afternoons walking in the near-by town. Tea is at 4 p.m., and now it is dark at that time. After tea we read or play cards till dinner, at 7.30. After dinner some music. By the way, we have a ragtime band, composed of a piano, a snare drum, two sets of bones, a triangle and brass cymbals, and an auto horn. It is ' some ' band. We all go to bed fairly early."

Patrick was transferred to H.E. on December 29, 1917, to take up an appointment in the Training Division of the Air Board—as it was then—

and Major B. F. Moore, Royal Warwickshire Regiment and R.F.C., was given the command.

It was about this time, also, that General Trenchard went home to become Chief of the Air Staff, prior to the official formation of the Royal Air Force by the amalgamation of the R.F.C. and R.N.A.S. His successor to the command of the R.F.C. in the field was General Sir J. Salmond, who remained in this position till the end of the war.

January 1918 passed fairly quietly. Morey collided in the air with an Albatros scout during a fight and both pilots must have been killed, but as this was some way over the lines, we never heard the German pilot's fate. Up to this time, the Huns had been very good in sending information about the fate of our pilots, nor were we behind them in courtesy. On one occasion, during May 1917, a message was dropped on Douai aerodrome, two hours after his capture, announcing the safety of a German scout pilot whom we had driven down near St. Pol. A study of the lists sent over by the Germans showed that just over 50 per cent. of our missing airmen were alive—wounded or injured most probably—but alive. Later, after March 1918, these amenities were not so nicely observed and information became harder to get. February came and went with the squadron still at Marie Capelle. A. C. Ball, brother of Albert Ball, was missing on the 5th of this month. He was a very promising young officer, but it was too

early in his flying career to say that he would
have rivalled his brother. Happily he is alive,
and was repatriated at the end of the war.
Lieuts. H. Crompton and W. Duncan, 2/Lieuts. H.
Hegarty and V. Priestly may perhaps be mentioned as fighting most pluckily and well during
this month. Soden, by now a flight commander,
did a good show on February 5, 1918. He
attacked an Albatros scout, which he drove
down out of control, and was then attacked by
two other hostile machines, who drove him down
from 15,000 to 50 feet, eight miles over the line ;
he came back " hedge-hopping " and banking
round trees, and when halfway home saw the
leading Hun crash into a tree ; he then began
to gain on the other, and, finally outdistancing
him, crossed the trenches, still at 50 feet, and
came home.

On February 18, Hammersley, Clark, Evans,
and Kent took on four triplanes and got three of
them, Evans and Clark sharing one, and Kent
and Hammersley taking one each.

During the last month, before moving south,
a lot of work was done, and a great many bombs
were dropped from a low altitude on rest billets
and other targets, this form of annoying the Hun
having become fashionable.

Another unusual incident occurred when W.
Kent opened fire, one day in March, at an enemy
scout with both guns from a distance of about 400
yards. Usually it was considered complete waste

of ammunition to shoot at ranges exceeding 100 yards, while 10 or 15 yards was the really effective distance. This scout caught fire all right, however, and crashed in our lines. Bishop did a similar thing once in the summer of 1917, but it was not a practice that was encouraged.

Hammersley was still doing very well, while J. A. Duncan, H. D. Crompton, and J. S. Griffiths were all prominent during March. H. H. Balfour, now commanding a flight in 43, but an original member of 60, was adequately maintaining the high standard which was expected of one who had served in the squadron.

The S.E.5A., with which the squadron was equipped from July 1917 till the Armistice, deserves some description. A single-seater fighting scout, it was armed with a Lewis gun mounted on the top plane like the Nieuport, but carried, in addition, a Vicker's firing through the propeller. Its speed, with the 200 h.p. Hispano engine, would reach 130 miles per hour near the ground and was, in consequence, at least 25 miles per hour faster than the Nieuport. This increase of speed made a great difference, as it meant that the enemy could not run away, and, further, that the S.E.5, if caught at a disadvantage, could outdistance its adversaries. Against the advantage gained in speed by this change must be set off a certain loss in respect of power to manœuvre quickly, but, in spite of this, the change was very greatly to the pilot's advantage.

Every machine has its strong and its weak points, and though at first we found the S.E. heavy on the controls and sluggish on her turns, and though some were inclined to regret the silver Nieuports, yet we soon found that the former was a far better fighting instrument. In actual weight the S.E., when fully loaded (including the pilot), was about 700 lb. heavier than the Nieuport — roughly 2,000 lb. as against 1,300 lb. The new machine, too, was distinctly more difficult to land, as the under-carriage was relatively a good deal weaker, and, owing to the extra weight, she would run on much farther on the ground.

During the first few months, therefore, a great many machines were crashed on the aerodrome, more particularly after leaving Izel le Hameau, which was a beautiful landing ground, and moving to Marie Capelle, where there was not nearly so much room. There were more crashes in this period than we had had since the days of the Morane "bullets," and from this point of view we often regretted the little Nieuport, which a good pilot could put down on a postage stamp any-where.

CHAPTER V

THE MARCH OFFENSIVE (1918)

ALTHOUGH this chapter treats of the events of March 1918 and after, the following letters, which were written some months earlier, and are all by Molesworth, are reprinted below because they give an accurate picture at first hand of the feelings and emotions of a scout pilot. It must be remembered that these, as well as the preceding letters by the same hand, were all written in the Field, and that they have not been altered or touched up in any way.

The author, who is a regular soldier, has now returned to his regiment, the Royal Munster Fusiliers, but all who knew him in 60 hope that the future expansion of the Air Force will draw him back before long to the service in which he fought so well.

"60 SQUADRON R.F.C.,
"B.E.F., FRANCE.
"*June* 1917.

" There is no doubt that scout pilots have the most exciting experiences while flying over Hunland, and it sometimes happens that these experiences may be their last. Always they are face to face with death in one form or another, always the thread suspending the 'sword of Damocles' may break and they may be hurled into eternity. However, we do not think of these sort of things in the air, but instead, we are filled with the spirit of confidence in our machines, and the ever-present thought that the best way to defend is to attack.

" There is the feeling of joy about it all which is sometimes mixed with loneliness. You are flying between a huge expanse of earth or sea below, merging into the vast spaces of the heavens above. The continuous drone of the engine in front of you and the whistling of the wind through the wires all add to this sense of loneliness, while the bracing air, and the knowledge that you have some of the finest machines and companions in the patrol, make you feel that flying is absolute perfection.

" Sometimes, however, you have a rude awakening, either in the form of a ' wop ' from Archie, or the ' rat-tat-tat-tat ' of a watchful enemy's machine gun, or again a sickening check in the rhythmic beat of your engine.

" This last experience happened to me a few days ago when I was leading a patrol of five machines about three miles over Hunland, at 12,000 feet. No Huns seemed to be about. Either Archie had forgotten our existence, or there was too much ground mist for him to see us. It was a perfect day up top, with a few light

clouds floating about. Away to the north-east
we could just distinguish the town of Douai,
while far below us the intricate system of the
Hindenburg Line, with its Drocourt-Quéant
Switch, stretched like a great ' T ' over the
shell-marked country.

" We were cruising along quietly, doing about
1,050 revolutions, when suddenly there was a
shattering noise in front of me, and I saw my
cowling break away in bits. Parts of it went
through the planes, luckily doing no vital damage.
Of course the engine stopped dead, and so I had
to put her nose down for home. It was quite
impossible to reach any of our aerodromes, so I
made towards Bapaume, keeping my eyes open for
a good landing ground all the time. The needle
on my altitude dial began to drop —11,000, 10,000,
9,000 —with corresponding wind-up on my part,
until we were about 2,000 feet from the ground.
I knew it meant a crash if I didn't make a good
landing, as the engine was absolutely *hors de
combat*. Suddenly I caught sight of a Bessoneau
hangar,[1] and near it an F.E. Bird perched on the
ground. I did a side-slip,[2] and landed into
wind, putting the machine down with rather a
bump ; however, there was nothing seriously
damaged. Luckily the wind was blowing from

---

[1] A type of hangar invented by a Frenchman and generally used
on our aerodromes in France.

[2] A method used to bring a machine down quickly without
gaining speed.

the north, otherwise I don't think I could ever have got across the lines.

" It turned out that the place where I had landed was an advanced F.E.8 landing ground.

" After going over my engine, I found that a tappet rod had broken and stripped the cowling. I telephoned over to the aerodrome and told them to bring out a spare engine and cowl. They soon arrived, and had the machine ready for me by the afternoon, so I pushed off home and arrived safely back soon after."

" 60 Squadron R.F.C.,
"B.E.F., France.
" *June* 1917.

" The heat is simply terrific, and the only ways of keeping cool are flying or sitting under the trees in the orchard. We spend most of the day, when not in the air, in multi-coloured pyjamas, some lads even going so far as to fly in them.

" Another awfully good way of keeping cool is to dig a hole about a foot deep and 3 feet long and cover it with a ground-sheet, pegged down at the corners, so as to make a bath. You lie in this with a book and a cooling drink by your side, and if you are lucky enough to escape the bombardment of mud, stones, and various other missiles which are thrown at you by the more energetic and lively spirits in the camp, you can really enjoy yourself. These baths have been such a success that we decided to dig a small bathing-pool about 20 feet square by 3 feet deep. When we got this going the whole population of the nearest village had to come and watch us. This was rather disconcerting, as we used to bathe *tout à fait nude*. Most of the chaps managed to rig up something in the way of a bathing-dress by buying various articles of clothing in the neighbouring village —I was forced to content myself with a type of female undergarment, which seemed to cause great amusement amongst the ack-emmas.[1]

" The village maidens were highly delighted, and thought it quite the thing, now that we were decently clad, to watch us at our aquatic sports.

" We three flight commanders have decided to take over a Nissen hut and knock out the partition so as to make it into one room ; of course, some wags had to start painting things on the outside. They began by printing on the window in large black letters, ' Saloon Bar ' ; and ended by naming the hut the ' Hôtel du Commerce,' as most of the squadron seemed to collect there, including Kate and Black Boy (the special pet dogs of the squadron), who made it their abode.

" I don't think I told you in my last letter that one of my pilots nearly finished me off. I was leading a patrol, when, without any warning, he dived about four yards in front of me. We would have collided if I hadn't managed to yank my machine over on her back. He successfully put

---

[1] Air mechanics.

the wind up me, I can tell you, and I gave it to him pretty hot when we got down."

" 60 Squadron R.F.C.,
"B.E.F., France.
"*June* 1917.

" I hope it will be ' dud ' to-morrow, as I want to supervise the painting of my grids. We have all got the craze of having them coloured. Mine are going to have red, white, and blue wheels. Our crack flight commander [1] has had a spinner made and painted blue, which he says puts the wind up the Huns. I should think they must be getting to know him well now, as he has crashed twenty-five of them, two of which he got in flames yesterday. He always lets us know when he has got one by firing a red Very light over the aerodrome before landing.

" Talking about colours, you ought to see the Huns. They are just like butterflies, with bright red bodies, spotted wings, and black and white squares on their tails, or else a wonderful mauve colour with green and brown patches.

" It was our day off yesterday, so the Major [2] asked me to go for a ride with him. We borrowed horses from a cavalry depot near-by, and set out in his car for the rendezvous where we were to pick them up. We did not intend to go far, but lost our way in a wood. The Major is a keen horseman and, consequently, led me over all sorts of obstacles, such as fallen trees, etc. Not having

---

[1] Bishop.   [2] Scott.

ridden for three years, I found it rather a job to stick on ; however, I got used to it. We went up and down vertical banks, and eventually had to get the nags over a 3-foot jump, which we managed to do with a bit of coaxing. Soon after we arrived at the beautiful old château of Lucheux, where we were to meet the car. This château was used by Marlborough during the Flanders Wars. It is now a Red Cross hospital. We had a talk to the sisters, and wangled some topping roses out of them for the mess. The car was waiting for us, so we got into it and drove home.

" When we arrived back, we found the mess decorated with branches of trees, which made it look like a greenhouse. This was to commemorate the Major's M.C., which he has just been awarded for bringing down Huns. We had a tremendous ' bust ' in the evening in which the Major joined. Speeches were made wishing him the best of luck, and then we retired to the ante-room and had a good old rag."

" 60 SQUADRON R.F.C.,
" B.E.F., FRANCE.
" *July* 1917.

"Rotten luck !

" Everything is black to-day. The Major [1] has been wounded in the arm ; one of my best pilots [2] is going off to another squadron as a flight commander, and I missed an absolute ' sitter ' this morning on our side of the line. However,

---

[1] Scott. [2] G. L. Lloyd.

every cloud has a silver lining. This time it is in the shape of an M.C. for one of our flight commanders who thoroughly deserves it. He hasn't managed to get a big bag yet, but there is lots of the ' good stuff ' in him, in both senses of the word.

" We are going to have a great ' bust ' to-night to commemorate it, and to cheer things up a bit. The show on which the Major was hit was a pretty hot mix-up. We were in the middle of our tennis tournament when word came through that a large formation of Huns was on the line. It was ' A ' Flight's turn for a job, so they pushed off, accompanied by the Major. They got into a big ' dog-fight,' and a Hun, who wasn't in the show at all, took a pot shot at long range and hit the Major in the arm, breaking up his switch at the same time. However, he managed to get back to the aerodrome all right, and went off to hospital soon after.

" We got into another big show on the 11th, and scrapped hard for about twenty minutes over the Hindenburg Line, without any luck. At last one of the Huns, with more guts than the rest, came over and began to attack one of our grids. I nipped in behind him without being seen and gave him a dose of lead. I must have hit his guns or something, as he had no ginger left, and simply flew west across the lines, intending to land on our side. Of course, my stupid old gun had to stop, and I discovered, to my annoyance, that there was no ammunition left. Seeing that I didn't fire, the

Hun guessed that something was up and turned back. I felt absolutely wild to see him calmly sneak off into a cloud on his way home.

" On another occasion, when three of us were attacking a formation of six Huns, one of us had a most extraordinary escape. We had our noses down, going full out to try and catch the blighters, when suddenly the Hun directly under us did a sharp turn. The chap on my right yanked his grid over after him. He pulled her over with such a jerk that one of his bottom planes came off and fluttered down to the ground in two bits. I couldn't see what happened to him after that, as we were getting to close quarters with the Huns. We tried to scrap them, but hadn't any luck, as they wouldn't put up a fight.

" When we arrived home, I reported that one of my patrol[1] had ' gone west,' as I had seen him break up in the air. Hardly had I finished when, to my amazement, he appeared outside the window. I could not believe my eyes and thought it was his ghost, but he turned out to be flesh and blood, and so we went to the mess and had a drink on the strength of it.

" He told me that he had managed to fly his kite back with great difficulty. Luckily the top planes had held. Of course, when he landed, the machine turned over and crashed, but he crawled out unhurt.

" We three flight commanders went to see the

[1] Penny.

Major in hospital yesterday. He seemed in the best of spirits, and had been trying to ' pump ' a Hun observer, who was in his ward, by asking him whether he liked doing artillery work on our part of the front, but the old Boche wouldn't give him an answer.

" We all hope to have the Major back with us soon, as his arm is much better. We miss him ' some,' as he often comes with us on our patrols.

" Charlie Chaplin isn't in it now with us ! We were cinematographed the other day. Some of us stood in a row and tried to look pleasant and unconcerned, but this was rather difficult, as everyone else was making rude remarks about us. We then bundled into our new grids, which we have just got, and started off on a stunt formation, nearly running down the old cinema man to put the wind up him. After we had done a circuit, my radiator began to boil, and I was forced to come down. Thank heavens! it was a good landing, as the old man was still at it turning the handle. My part of the show was to be known as ' Pilot landing for more ammunition after fierce fight.' "

"60 Squadron R.F.C.,
"B.E.F., France.
"*August* 1917.

" The new grids [1] are a great success, and we have been hard at work training and doing line patrols.

" Three of us, led by our famous ' Hun-strafer,' [2]

[1] The S.E.5s.   [2] Bishop.

used them over the lines for the first time on the
5th. As a rule we only fight in flights, but on
certain occasions we volunteer for a ' circus,' that
is a mixed formation generally composed of the
best pilots in the squadron.

" Our numbers were not overwhelming this
time, but we know that the Huns had got pukka
wind-up by the way they disappeared when we
arrived on the line, so we felt quite confident in
taking on twice as many as ourselves. Of course
we were all out for trouble, as we wanted to show
what the new machines could do. As soon as our
leader spotted a formation of Huns, he was after
them like a flash. I think there were seven of
them, but we were all much too excited to count.
Suddenly they saw us coming, and tried des-
perately to escape, but our leader got into his
favourite position, and the rear Hun hadn't a
ghost of a chance. The next instant he was a
flaming mass.

" We simply had it all over the Boche for speed
and, as we had the height, they could not possibly
get away. I picked my man out as he was coming
towards me, and dived straight at him, opening
fire with both guns at close range. He suffered
the same fate as his companion.

" A burning machine is a glorious but terrible
sight to see—a tiny red stream of flame trickles
from the petrol tank, then long tongues of blazing
petrol lick the sides of the fuselage, and, finally,
a sheet of white fire envelops the whole machine,

and it glides steeply towards the ground in a zigzag course, leaving a long trail of black smoke behind it, until it eventually breaks up. There is no doubt that your first Hun in flames gives you a wonderful feeling of satisfaction. I can well imagine what the big-game hunter must think when he sees the dead lion in front of him. Somehow, you do not realise that you are sending a man to an awful doom, but rather your thoughts are all turned on the hateful machine which you are destroying, so fascinating to look at and yet so deadly in its attack."

> " 60 SQUADRON R.F.C.,
> " B.E.F., FRANCE.
> " *August* 1917.

" Sorry I haven't written for some time, but we have been kept awfully busy as the weather has been so fine. I have been trying hard to get another Hun, and only succeeded the day before yesterday, when we had another great scrap.

" Five of us met eight Huns and attacked them the other side of the line. I missed my man in the first dive, but turned on another and must have hit the pilot, as he spun straight into the ground. One of my patrol also destroyed an Albatros by shooting him up so that he fell to bits in the air. The remaining six Huns put up quite a good fight, and nearly got one of us by doing in his lateral control. However, he managed to land all right, as these machines are fairly stable.

" On scanning my kite, I discovered that it had not escaped scot-free, as a large piece of the tail plane had been shot away.

" There was tremendous excitement in the squadron yesterday, as our ' stunt merchant ' [1] has been awarded the V.C. for that aerodrome show that I told you about. We celebrated it last night by one of the finest ' busts ' I have ever had. There were speeches and lots of good ' bubbly,' consequently everyone was in the best of spirits.

"After dinner we had a torchlight procession to the various squadrons stationed on the aerodrome. This was led by our Very light experts. Luckily for us, the night was very dull and cloudy, or else I expect old man Boche would have had a hand in it too. We charged into one mess and proceeded to throw everyone and everything we came across out of the window. We then went over to the other squadron. The wretched lads were all in bed, but we soon had them out, and bombarded their mess with Very lights, the great stunt being to shoot one in through one window and out at the other. I can't imagine why the blessed place didn't go up in flames. After annoying these people for a bit, we retired to our own mess, where we danced and sang till the early hours of the morning. I have still got a piece of plaid cloth about 6 inches square, which was the only thing left of a perfectly

[1] Bishop.

good pair of 'trouse' that belonged to one of our Scotch compatriots.

"This morning the C.O. sent for me to go to the orderly room. He told me that my name had come through for H.E.,[1] and congratulated me on having been awarded the M.C.

"Later I went round to the sheds to say good-bye to the men, and finally ended up at the mess to have a farewell drink with all my old friends.

"I can hardly realise that the time has come for me to go back to Blighty. I shall be awfully bucked to see you again in a few days, old chap, and yet I can't help feeling sad at leaving this dear old place—full of memories, sometimes tragic, sometimes comic. It is very hard to part with these comrades of mine—'Knights of the Air,' who live from day to day facing eternity with a smile, and laying down their lives, if need be, with such heroism, for the cause of freedom."

*   *   *   *   *

To return to the squadron which we left at Marie Capelle. On March 8, 1918, orders arrived to move up to Bailleul—a good deal nearer the line —where they remained for over a fortnight. This aerodrome was shelled every day that they were there, and on the last two nights was heavily bombed. On March 27 they were rushed down to Bellevue, near Doullens, to cope with the offensive which, as few will have forgotten, began on the 21st. This move brought the squadron back into

[1] Home Establishment.

the 13th Wing, in which it served, except for the winter of 1917–18, during the whole of its career on the Western Front.   After three days at Belle-vue another move was ordered to Fienvilliers.

On March 30, in the course of one patrol, Hammersley, the leader, destroyed two Hun scouts, putting one on to the roof of a house in Hem, where it burst into flames ; while Copeland, Hegarty, Duncan, and Griffiths all shot down hostile machines, the destruction of which was officially confirmed.   Bartlett also shot down one out of control.   Both Copeland and Duncan were now piling up good scores.

On April 12 there was yet another move, this time to Boffles, where they stayed until September.   For some time past they had been in tents, ready to move at a moment's notice, and by now all the household goods which a squadron ac-cumulated during the period of stationary warfare had disappeared : the bronze figures and silver basins, brought back as mementoes (on payment) after celebrations in Amiens and elsewhere ; the original of Fleming Williams' picture of a Nieuport scout ; the cut-glass reproductions of two of his father's valuable decanters, presented to the squadron by Lord Dalmeny on his departure for Egypt with General Allenby ; the German sign-boards, shell-cases, and other trophies ; all had been left behind or were lost long before the March retreat and the subsequent victorious advance were over.   This was a pity, but could not be helped.

The losses of the Air Force during this retreat were very heavy indeed. Usually we used to calculate that the Germans lost twice as many machines as the British, according to the reports issued by our Headquarters. This thought was a comforting one. Under the head of hostile machines destroyed are not included, for the purpose of this calculation, those shown as driven down out of control. It should be remembered that Headquarters required very clear confirmation before officially recognising the destruction of an enemy machine, and that many Huns must have been destroyed which were not counted. If one set fire to a Boche machine in the air there was no difficulty, as the whole sky saw it and confirmation was readily forthcoming ; but where this was not done, it was not at all easy to watch the victim glide down from fifteen or sixteen thousand feet, and to mark the spot at which he crashed. It takes a long time to reach the ground from nearly three miles up, and there were always plenty of watchful enemies in the sky waiting to swoop on to the overkeen pilot who forgot everything but his presumably vanquished foe. Once a pilot took his eyes off a machine, it was by no means always easy to pick it up again. The best type was always careful not to claim a doubtful Hun, and, though there were plenty who would like to have done so, the other officers of the flight generally knew pretty well when a doubtful claim was put in, and soon gave the offender a hint that such conduct did the squadron no good. It may, therefore, fairly be assumed that we had destroyed the full number of machines claimed. The German method of calculation was somewhat different, as they counted a two-seater machine as two " victories," which made their star pilots appear to be more successful than ours.

Throughout the war, on the Western Front, the policy of the R.F.C., as directed by General Sir Hugh Trenchard, was that our fighters should engage the enemy over his territory and never allow him to cross our lines. These orders were never executed with complete success, as it is not possible to erect and maintain an aerial barrage, so to speak, which can completely prevent a resolute pilot from penetrating it if he really means to do so, nor can it be said that our patrols kept, in every case, always on the other side of the line. Broadly speaking, however, we fought over alien territory, the Germans over their own. The effect of this was that many a British machine was forced to land, disabled by gunfire or through engine failure, and the occupants, even though unwounded, were lost to their own side till the end of the war. The German pilot, on the other hand, whose engine was put out of action in a fight might land safely, get another machine, and be fighting again the same day.

Another circumstance which, in fairness to the Air Force, should always be borne in mind when the conditions of fighting in the air are under discussion, is that on the Western Front the wind entered very much into all questions of aerial strategy or tactics.   The prevailing wind was that west wind which Conrad thus describes in a brilliant passage, and which, though it deals with the sea, is equally true of the air on the Western Front :

" The narrow seas around these isles, where British admirals keep watch and ward upon the marches of the Atlantic Ocean, are subject to the turbulent sway of the west wind.

" Call it north-west or south-west, it is all one— a different phase of the same character, a changed expression of the same face.   In the orientation of the winds that rule the seas, the north and south directions are of no importance.   The north and the south winds are but small princes in the dynasties that make peace and war upon the sea. In the polity of the winds, as among the tribes of the earth, the real struggle lies between east and west.   The end of the day is the time to gaze at the kingly face of the westerly weather, who is the arbiter of ships' destinies.

" Benignant and splendid, or splendid and sinister, the western sky reflects the hidden purpose of the royal wind.

" Clothed in a mantle of dazzling gold or draped in rags of black cloud like a beggar, the might of the westerly wind sits enthroned upon the western horizon, with the whole North Atlantic as a footstool for his feet and the first twinkling stars making a diadem for his brow.''

It was this powerful sovereign, this pitiless potentate who, five days out of seven, fought with our enemies against us, and it is to be hoped that he is properly humiliated by the result of the war. How many curses have been levelled at his careless head by pilots who, with trailing wires, with labouring, failing engines, and with tattered planes have tried, and often tried in vain, to reach that brown, smoky strip of battered terrain which marked the lines and safety, after a bitter fight ? How often has a patrol, on a day with the wind at fifty to sixty miles an hour, at 10,000 feet fought batch after batch of Huns when on the Mons-Maubeuge or some other '' long reconnaissance,'' only to find that, though every enemy may have been shot down in flames, though no black-crossed machines remained to smirch the sky, inexorable Zephyrus had swept them during the fight so far towards the Rhine that lack of petrol must force them to land on hostile ground ? Who has not felt, when turning homewards on a stormy day, that the machine could make no progress at all against the wind, but seemed for minutes that were like hours to stand still over some town or village ? Actually headway was as a rule being made, but the change in ground speed from flying down-wind to struggling against it produced this very powerful illusion, and pilots have often thrown their guns, ammunition, and even field-glasses overboard with the frantic hope of lightening the machine and thus increasing her speed.

No ! Zephyrus, who should have been a Teuton god, and who beyond question wears the Iron Cross, was no friend to the Air Force. We should perhaps have poured out libations to his eastern brothers—Eurus and Aquilus—or at very least have recommended them for the immediate award of the Distinguished Flying Cross in recognition of their invaluable services throughout the war.

The struggle wore on through May, and during the middle of this month the fighting in the air was terrific.

One hundred and thirty E.A. (enemy aircraft) were brought down by the Air Force in France between the 13th and 19th of the month. Belgrave and Scholte were, perhaps, the most successful, but I. M. Davies, A. W. Saunders, Hegarty, V. S. Griffith, W. A. Duncan, were also very prominent. During one patrol, led by Belgrave on June 12, in which he shot down a two-seater, R. G. Lewis, whose engine presumably had failed, went down and landed, breaking his under-carriage. H. A. Gordon, a Canadian whose first trip over the lines this was, landed beside him and got out of his own machine. At this point some soldiers appeared and opened fire. Gordon ran back to his S.E., calling to

Lewis to get in with him, but the latter, apparently mistaking the troops for friends, walked towards them. Gordon then took off and circled round, meaning to fire, but, seeing Lewis in the midst of them, refrained, and returned home with his machine very badly shot about. He was killed two months later.

An S.E.5 has carried two before now, but it is an unpleasant experience for the passenger, who has to sit with his legs on each side of the pilot's shoulders and to hold on to the top gun-mounting.

By this time, Bishop was back in France commanding No. 85 Squadron and was doing wonders. Much of his success was due now, as always, to his extremely accurate shooting, the importance of which in aerial fighting it is almost impossible to exaggerate.

W. H. Saunders did a very good show on July 2, fighting continuously for forty-five minutes, destroying two Pfalz scouts and engaging five other hostile machines.

At the beginning of July, Barry Moore was promoted to command No. 1 Aeroplane Supply Depot at Marquise, and J. B. McCudden, V.C., D.S.O., M.C., was appointed to succeed him in the command of the squadron. While flying down to take over from Moore, he got his machine into a spin near the ground, crashed, and was killed. Though he never actually joined 60, and though this history is concerned only to describe the exploits of that squadron, a paragraph must, nevertheless, be devoted to McCudden's achievements. He joined the R.F.C. as an air mechanic before the war, fought as an N.C.O. pilot with 29 Squadron during 1916–17, was then given a commission and was posted to 56 Squadron, where he specialised in two-seaters, that variety of two-seater which the Germans would send over very high at 20,000 feet or more on clear days to photograph our back areas, and which were not easy to bring down. The difficulty was that they were first seen, as a rule, at a great height, and our fighting machines had to climb up to them, which would take fifteen minutes at least. During this interval which necessarily elapsed before the attacking machines could get their height, the Rumpler or L.V.G., which would be flying level, could usually outdistance the pursuers; if, however, the British machine contrived, by flying the inside of the circle, to keep between the Hun and the lines, the latter, if he was as cunning as they usually were, would calmly continue his photography while his adversary was climbing until the latter was about 1,500 feet below him, and, when his pursuer was getting close enough to be dangerous, would put his nose down slightly, open up his engine and disappear into Hunland, leaving a streak of blue smoke, but nothing more tangible, behind him.

McCudden, however, with great resolution and infinite patience, studied the habits of these folk and shot down dozens of them. In addition, he

8

was a brilliant and successful patrol leader and one whom the Air Force could ill spare. After his death, C. M. Crowe, M.C., who also had a fine record both in 56 Squadron and, earlier in the war, with other units, was given the command. After a few weeks, Crowe had a serious motor accident and was " struck off " the strength, to be posted later to 85 Squadron. He was succeeded by A. C. Clarke, an old Etonian, who remained in charge till the end of the war.

On August 1, 60, together with 3, 56, and 11 Squadrons, carried out an extremely successful raid on Epinoy Aerodrome. Sixteen machines were believed to have been destroyed as a result of this operation and two large fires were started, the smoke of which ascended to a height of over 10,000 feet.   60 and 11 did the " upper guard," escorting 3 and 56, who went down and actually shot up the aerodrome, whilst the two former squadrons kept off hostile machines who might have attacked the raiders from above.

Raids of this kind were most successful, but had only lately become possible on account of the much larger number of squadrons which were now available. Up to this time, the number of machines had been only just sufficient to get through the ordinary routine work, i.e. low flying on battle days, offensive patrols for the indirect protection of the artillery machine, by the destruction of the enemy scouts who would have interfered with them, and escorts to bombing raids and photographic reconnaissances. These last two duties the improved types of two-seater fighters now carried out without escorts—the De Havilland 4s, 9s, and Bristol fighters being quite capable of operating without protection by scouts.

During August, R. K. Whitney (who had had a great month in July), Doyle, G. M. Duncan, Buckley, and A. W. Saunders (who was now a flight commander), were all fighting well. One patrol led by the last-named on August 9 accounted for four enemy aircraft.

Lieut. A. Beck now rejoined the squadron : he had been with us in June 1917, but was sent home on the representation of his parents, who complained that he was only seventeen. Returning a year later, he speedily showed that his youth was no disqualification. He remained with the squadron till the end, was promoted flight commander, and did extraordinarily good work.

On August 8 we assumed the offensive east of Amiens. 60 did a great deal of low flying and low bombing, as well as the usual " scrapping " up above. The Fokker biplane D.7 first appeared in numbers at this time. This was an original type of machine without any external wiring but with a very thick wing section, which was braced internally. Its performance was very good, alike as regards speed, climb, and power to manœuvre. Their pilots were usually provided with parachutes, which quite often failed to open. From all along the line reports now came in showing that the use of the parachute was becoming fairly general among German pilots.

In October, while our advance was proceeding, squadrons of the Air Force dropped some thousands of boxes of rations and ammunition for Belgian troops, whose supplies had been held up owing to the speed of the advance. 60, however, took no part in this.

H. C. M. Orpen, I. W. Rayner, S. V. Mason, M. D. Sinclair, O. P. Johnson, G. M. Duncan, and McEntegart were, perhaps, the most prominent and successful pilots during the British advance, which was a time of continuous and sustained effort on the part of every officer, N.C.O., and man in the whole squadron. The strain of sending at least two full-strength squadron patrols daily over the line, while moving continually, severely taxed the endurance of all ranks. They left Boffles for Baisieux on September 17, Baisieux for Beugnatre on October 14, and finally moved from the latter station to Quievy, an old German aero‹ drome, on October 31.

By October the Air Force mechanical transport had begun to wear out, nor is this surprising when the work it had done is remembered; the men were always working hard to keep the lorries and light tenders on the road. Moreover, the new aerodromes were always pitted with shell-holes, which had to be filled up, and scarcely was this task completed before orders would arrive to move again. In spite of these difficulties, the supplies of rations, ammunition, etc., were maintained with wonderful regularity by the H.Q. staffs.

The German Flying Corps continued to fight hard and well up to the very last day of the war, and, though their armies on the ground were retreating fast, no signs of demoralisation in the air were observed.

During these last days, throughout September and October, a great deal of work was done with 148—an American Camel squadron—most of whose pilots had been trained in England. This unit was also in the 13th Wing, and the two squadrons moved forward together to the various aerodromes mentioned above. They did several good shows together, notably between September 14 and 17, during the attack on Havrincourt Wood, when 60 twice a day did the "upper guard," while 148 flew low, bombing troops and attacking low-flying Fokkers. A considerable amount of damage was done during the progress of these operations. For example, on September 26 one patrol of each squadron, working in the same manner, gave a good exhibition of combined work : 60's patrol, led by Rayner, drove down a flight of Fokkers into the jaws of 148, who tackled them with such effect that three were "crashed" and one driven down out of control. Again, on the next day, during the Bourlon Wood attack, 148, protected as before by 60, crashed two enemy two-seaters, the destruction of which was observed and confirmed by the latter unit.

During the whole of the advance towards Cambrai and beyond, the two squadrons did at least one " show " a day together until October 30, when the Americans left Beugnatre, near Bapaume, to go south to join their own army near Nancy, a very long and tiresome journey. On the day before leaving, their last patrol with us " crashed " either four or five Huns.

Their pilots were many of them trained at London Colney, in Hertfordshire, and Lieuts. Springs (who accounted for nine enemy machines), L. K. Callaghan (whose score when they left for Nancy was eight), and J. O. Creech (who had got six Huns), were all good advertisements for the methods adopted at that training station.

Other pilots conspicuous in this squadron were two of their flight commanders (T. Clay and F. E. Kindley) and also Lieut. C. T. McLean, all of whom will no doubt remember a dinner in Amiens, on October 18, in which 201 Squadron also joined with 60 in celebrating the turn of the tide in the Allied fortunes, a change which 148 and 17 American (this latter squadron was also in the 13th Wing) had certainly done their share to bring about.

There was great regret on the part of all their British comrades in arms when these two American units went away.

One of the pilots of 148, who had been taken

prisoner, told a remarkable story on his return just after the Armistice. This pilot, who had served with 56 Squadron, also in the 13th Wing, some months earlier, was shot down and, after having landed more or less safely in " Hunland," was taken before a German intelligence officer and asked his name and squadron. Having given his name and rank only, his examiner said to him, " But you were in 56—I dined with you in December last," and followed this up by asking the astonished prisoner if he did not remember a French Breguet (two-seater) landing at 56's aerodrome one day with an officer pilot and a mechanic on board. The American did remember, and recollected, too, that the pilot announced that he was coming up from the south to join a French squadron north of our 2nd Army near Dixmude, but that his engine was running badly and he had landed to make some adjustments. No one in 56 at this time knew very much about the French Flying Corps, but everyone knew that their machines had often passed over the intervening British armies in this manner, particularly during the summer of 1917, prior to the Passchendale battles, and again in April 1918, when Foch's strategical schemes involved the introduction into the middle of our 2nd Army area of a French division, which defended Kemmel Hill after the German break-through on the Lys. The story, therefore, appeared to be quite a natural one, and no one suspected for an instant that anything was wrong. The " repairs " to the 200 h.p. Renault engine, a type with which none of our mechanics were very familiar, took longer than was expected, and the " Frenchman " dined and stayed the night with the squadron, making himself most agreeable but refusing to drink much. Not only did he stay one night, but, the weather next day proving unfavourable, he remained a second, and on the third day flew off, it is believed, to another British aerodrome. There was no question of the truth of the story because the hero of it showed, when talking to his prisoner, a knowledge of the officers in 56, their appearance and nicknames, together with the details of the camp and aerodrome, which could only have been obtained at first-hand. Moreover, the American pilot remembered the visit quite well, and even recognised his interrogator. The German also told him that he had played the same game with the French Flying Corps, pretending, on a captured British machine, to be an English pilot making his way down to our Independent Air Force, which, under General Trenchard, was stationed opposite Metz, a long way from the nearest British unit.

It was easier for the Germans to do this kind of thing than it would have been for the Allies, owing to the duality of language on our side of the line ; but, nevertheless, it must be reckoned a very fine performance. Presumably, he left the German aerodrome before dawn and flew about on our side of the line until it was light enough to land, but, even so, he was lucky not to have been attacked on his return by German machines and anti-aircraft guns when flying an aeroplane with Allied markings, as it must have been impossible to warn the German aviators that one particular Breguet was not to be molested, mainly because of the impossibility of distinguishing one machine from another of the same type in the air, but also because to circulate general instructions of this kind would almost certainly have given the whole plan away to some of the Allied agents who, on the whole, were much more efficient than the German spies.

After the Armistice, when the question of demobilisation began to be considered in the Air Force and particulars of the terms of each officer's engagement were scrutinised, it was surprising to find how many Americans were serving in English scout squadrons. There seemed to be at least three or four American citizens in each single-seater squadron in France, out of a total in such a squadron of twenty-five officers. Moreover, the majority of these wore at least one medal for gallantry, the reason being, no doubt, that these young men were the very flower of the American fighting stock, who felt unable to wait until their country came into the war, but represented themselves to be Canadian citizens in order to join in the contest. Had the war lasted a little longer, most of them would, no doubt, have transferred to their own squadrons, as some few had already done, but at the end of 1918 their own air effort had not yet developed sufficiently to absorb them all.

To return, however, to 60. The squadron's last " confirmed Hun " of the war was secured on November 1 by Capt. A. Beck, who had lately destroyed, when flying low, a number of enemy artillery observation machines (two-seaters).

The arrival at Quievy, halfway between Cambrai and Le Cateau, where the squadron remained until after the signing of the Armistice, was most interesting. Here remained some of the German semi-permanent hangars, the machine-gun emplacements on the roofs of the houses surrounding the aerodrome, and here, too, were people who for four and a half long years had lived with the pilots and observers of the German Flying Corps. The questions asked by our officers—usually in extremely moderate French—were endless. " How many jobs a day did they do ? " " Were their casualties heavy ? " " Were the pilots usually officers or N.C.O.s ? " " How many machines did they have in a flight ? " are only a few examples. The answers in most cases were disappointing, as the Boche seemed to have taken good care to keep all civilians off his aerodromes.

The plight of the inhabitants of the occupied territory was wretched ; the retreating enemy had driven off every single head of livestock, taking even the poultry away over the Belgian border, and the British forces had to feed them for many weeks until the French lorry services began to

work and until the railways were restored.

Delay-action mines were left everywhere in this part of the world, though there were not, perhaps, as many booby traps as were found after the Boche retreat of March 1917 to the Hindenburg or Wotan Line.   The bridge at Caudry station, the railhead from which the squadron drew rations, went up on November 1, killing and wounding twenty or thirty men.

The uncultivated state of the land was very noticeable in this district; for though some poor root and winter cabbage crops showed here and there, grown by the inhabitants under German direction, most of the fields did not appear to have been tilled at all, though this particular tract had been a long way behind the line until August 1918.

The last few days' fighting were marked by no unusual incidents so far as 60 itself was concerned, though it was thrilling to be forming part of the army which was retaking Valenciennes, Le Quesnoy, Maubeuge, and other towns immediately in front of us.   Thrilling, too, to see the long dingy columns, already in Belgium, marching east at last.

On Armistice night, Clarke hurriedly organised a dinner, to which such old members as were in the neighbourhood were bidden.   It was a good evening, ending with the invasion of the officers' mess by the N.C.O.s and men, who drank each other's healths—not that there was overmuch alcohol available—and sang over and over again

those very ordinary music-hall songs which our
people always seem to employ as a medium for
expression in moments of emotional stress.
Officers and men bellowed together " The good
ship Yacki Hicki Doola " and similar classics.

60 was always remarkable for the cordial
relations between the officers and men, due,
perhaps, to the fact that an Air Force scout
squadron during the war was, in Lord Hugh
Cecil's words, " a natural aristocracy," in that the
officers flew and fought twice daily while the men
remained on the ground in comparative security.

CHAPTER VI

DEMOBILISATION

THE latter half of November and the first week of December was a period of suspense. No one quite knew what was to happen, nor did the first circulars on the subject, even the famous one beginning, " And Joshua bade the people disperse every man to his own place," clear up the situation very much. It was not, in fact, until Mr. Churchill had been appointed Secretary of State for War and Air, and had laid down the broad principle that men over thirty-five and those who had enlisted before January 1, 1916, were to be allowed to go and that the rest must stay, that we knew where we were at all. It was difficult, also, to find employment from day to day for the men. Association football, however, was always popular, concerts and boxing contests were frequently held, while horses and dogs were borrowed and hare-hunting was attempted.

One form of hare-hunting became very popular the idea—which originated with Louis Strange, then commanding a wing—was to proceed as follows: All officers and men in the wing who wished to take part assembled, to the number of

two or three hundred, at " the meet," and filed
away in opposite directions, the leaders of each
file turning gradually inwards until a circle
nearly a mile in diameter was enclosed by men
about twenty yards apart. The circle being
completed, they began to walk towards the
centre. Usually three or four hares, and sometimes many more, got up within the cordon and
ran frantically round until they either broke
through or were knocked over with sticks. The
shouting and noise arising during the proceedings
testified to the popularity of this form of sport.
Despite these diversions, time hung rather heavily
on their hands until, at last, by the end of February
1919, all the demobilisable officers and men had
gone, and those who remained were sent up by
train as reinforcements to the R.A.F. with the
Army of the Rhine. On a bitterly cold evening
this remnant entrained in covered trucks, under
sad skies with snow falling heavily, to commence
their eastward journey, in typically military
fashion, by travelling due west to Etaples. After
this nothing remained but to dispatch the cadre
with the records back to England, and the two
officers and ten men remaining accordingly departed on February 28, bound for Sedgeford, in
Norfolk.

The squadron remained dormant for a time, but
was re-formed towards the end of the year, and is
now equipped with De Havilland 10s, large twin-
engined machines, and is stationed in India.

Most of the officers and men are new, but such veterans as are available will be drafted back when circumstances allow, and there is no old member of the squadron who is not confident that the new formation will add to that high reputation which 60 has enjoyed from the day of its birth, and which we, who served in it, have helped to build, or, at all events, have tried our hardest not to damage.

Though the records, owing to a fire in the squadron office in November 1916, may perhaps be not quite complete, yet the destruction of 274 enemy aircraft can be traced.

The honours gained by officers or men, whilst serving in the squadron, are :

> 1 V.C.
> 5 D.S.O.s.
> 1 Bar to D.S.O.
> 37 Military Crosses.
> 5 Distinguished Flying Crosses.

The map which will be found at the end of this chapter is published by permission of Field-Marshal Earl Haig, and shows very clearly the ground gained and the prisoners taken by the victorious British armies during the last three months of the war.

APPENDIX I

LIST OF OFFICERS WHO HAVE SERVED IN 60 SQUADRON

TOGETHER WITH THE DECORATIONS GAINED BY THEM,
NOT NECESSARILY IN THE SQUADRON ; ALL OFFICERS
ARE SHOWN IN THE HIGHEST RANK TO WHICH THEY
ATTAINED DURING THE WAR

Name.	Casualty.	Date.
2/Lieut. A. R. Adam	Missing	July 1917
Lieut. J. R. Anderson	Killed	Aug. 1918
Capt. D. V. Armstrong, D.F.C. (151 Sqdn.) .	Killed	May 1916
Lieut. J. L. Armstrong	—	Jan. 1918
Lieut. (A/Capt.) F. L. Atkinson . . .	Injured	April 1917
2/Lieut. W. R. Ayling	—	Nov. 1918
Lieut. J. Baalman	—	Aug. 1917
Lieut. D. H. Bacon	Missing	Nov. 1916
Lieut. C. G. Baker	—	Jan. 1917
Major H. H. Balfour, M.C. and Bar, Croix de Guerre (French)	—	May 1916
Capt. A. Ball, V.C., D.S.O. and 2 Bars, M.C., Order of St. George (Russian, 4th Class), Croix de Chevalier (French) . .	Killed	Sept. 1916
Lieut. A. C. Ball	Missing	Feb. 1918
Lieut. H. J. O. Barnett	—	Jan. 1918
Lieut. J. N. Bartlett	—	June 1918
F/Officer H. F. V. Battle . . .	Wounded	Sept. 1918
Capt. A. Beck, D.F.C.	—	June 1918
Capt. J. D. Belgrave, M.C. and Bar .	Missing	April 1918
Major A. D. Bell-Irving, M.C. and Bar, Croix de Guerre	Wounded	May 1916
2/Lieut. I. Bigood	—	May 1916
Capt. A. Binnie, M.C.	Missing	April 1917
Lieut.-Col. W. A. Bishop, V.C., D.S.O. and Bar, M.C., D.F.C., Croix de Chevalier, Legion of Honour, Croix de Guerre with Palm (French)	—	April 1917
Capt. C. T. Black	—	March 1917
Capt. C. L. Blake	—	June 1917
Lieut. R. C. W. Blessley (U.S. Air Service) .	Wounded	Sept. 1918

Name.	Casualty.	Date.
2/Lieut. F. Bower	Killed	April 1917
Lieut. H. S. Brackenbury	Injured	March 1917
Capt. N. A. Browning-Paterson . . .	Killed	May 1916
Capt. W. E. G. Bryant, M.B.E. . . .	Wounded	May 1916
Lieut. H. E. W. Bryning	—	June 1918
2/Lieut. H. Buckley	Wounded	Aug. 1918
2/Lieut. E. A. Burbidge	—	Sept. 1918
2/Lieut. C. M. H. M. Caffyn . . .	Killed	March 1917
Major K. L. Caldwell, M.C., D.F.C. and Bar, Croix de Guerre (Belgian) . . .	—	Jan. 1917
Lieut. K. T. Campbell	Died	June 1918
Lieut. L. H. T. Capel	—	Feb. 1918
Capt. C. W. Carleton, A.F.C. . . .	—	Dec. 1916
2/Lieut. W. M. Carlyle	Missing	Oct. 1916
Lieut. A. Carter, M.M.	—	Sept. 1917
2/Lieut. W. E. Cass	Died	Aug. 1916
Lieut. G. F. Caswell	Missing	Sept. 1918
Capt. J. C. A. Caunter	Missing	Oct. 1917
2/Lieut. L. C. Chapman	Missing	April 1917
Capt. L. S. Charles	Missing	July 1916
Capt. R. L. Chidlaw-Roberts, M.C. . .	—	Sept. 1917
2/Lieut. E. W. Christie	Missing	April 1918
Capt. S. Clare, M.B.E.	—	Jan. 1918
Capt. F. W. Clark, A.F.C.	—	Jan. 1918
2/Lieut. L. L. Clark	Killed	May 1916
2/Lieut. R. B. Clark	Died of Wounds	April 1917
Major A. C. Clarke	—	Aug. 1918
Lieut. J. H. Cock	Missing	April 1917
A/Capt. E. S. T. Cole, M C. . . .	—	Sept. 1916
Capt. J. Collier, D.F.C. (80 Sqdn.) . .	—	July 1917
Capt. W. H. K. Copeland . . .	—	March 1918
Lieut. G. F. Court	—	Nov. 1917
2/Lieut. G. B. Craig	Missing	Feb. 1918
Lieut. F. D. Crane	—	Jan. 1918
Capt. K. Crawford	Missing	April 1918
Lieut. H. D. Crompton	—	Sept. 1917
Lieut. (A/Capt.) J. B. Crompton. . .	—	Sept. 1917
Major C. M. Crowe, M.C., D.F.C. . .	—	July 1918
Lieut. C. F. Cunningham . . .	—	Jan. 1918
F/Lieut. A. P. V. Daly	—	Nov. 1916
Capt. I. Meredyth Davies . . .	—	April 1918
Lieut. W. B. Day	—	Oct. 1918
Capt. G. C. Dell-Clarke, M.C. . . .	Killed	July 1918
2/Lieut. E. W. C. Densham . . .	—	Sept. 1918
F/Lieut. G. W. Dobson, O.B.E. . .	—	Oct. 1916
Capt. J. E. Doyle, D.F.C. . . .	Missing	Sept. 1918
Lieut. L. Drummond	—	Aug. 1916
Capt. J. M. Drysdale.	Wounded	Aug. 1916
Lieut. G. L. Du Cros	—	June 1918
Capt. G. M. Duncan, D.F.C. . . .	—	Aug. 1918
Capt. W. J. A. Duncan, M.C and Bar. .	—	Nov. 1917
2/Lieut. (Hon. Lieut.) J. Elgood . .	—	July 1916
Lieut. G. F. Elliott	—	Sept. 1917

9

Name.	Casualty.	Date.
Lieut. J. McC. Elliott	Missing	April 1917
Lieut. C. D. Evans	—	Jan. 1918
2/Lieut. J. J. Fitzgerald	Missing	Oct. 1917
2/Lieut. H. T. Flintoft	—	July 1918
2/Lieut. J. H. Flynn	Killed	Sept. 1917
Major E. L. Foot, M.C.	—	Oct. 1916
2/Lieut. C. V. Forsyth	—	Nov. 1918
Lieut. C. W. France	—	Aug. 1918
Capt. W. M. Fry, M.C.	—	Jan. 1917
Capt. P. E. M. Le Gallais, A.F.C. . .	—	Aug. 1916
Lieut. W. P. Garnett	Missing	March 1917
Lieut. F. O. Gibbon	—	July 1917
Major E. J. L. W. Gilchrist, M.C., D.F.C. .	Wounded	Dec. 1916
Lieut. W. Gilchrist	Missing	May 1917
Capt. G. A. Giles	—	Jan. 1917
Lieut. H. Good	—	May 1916
Capt. F. E. Goodrich, M.C. . . .	Killed	Sept. 1916
Lieut. H. A. Gordon	Missing	July 1918
2/Lieut. R. J. Grandin	Missing	July 1917
Major E. P. Graves	Killed	March 1917
Hon. Capt. D. B. Gray, M.C. . . .	—	May 1916
F/Lieut. E. O. Grenfell, M.C., A.F.C. . .	Wounded	Dec. 1916
F/Officer J. S. Griffith, D.F.C. and Bar, Order of St. Vladimir, 4th Class . . .	Wounded	July 1918
2/Lieut. W. H. Gunner, M.C. . . .	Missing	July 1917
Capt. H. W. Guy, Croix de Guerre (Belgian)	—	June 1917
Lieut. C. S. Hall	Missing	April 1917
Lieut. J. G. Hall	Missing	Nov. 1918
Lieut. H. Hamer, A.F.C.	—	Feb. 1917
Capt. H. A. Hamersley, M.C. . . .	—	Sept. 1917
Lieut. H. T. Hammond	Missing	Sept. 1917
2/Lieut. L. P. Harlow	—	Nov. 1918
Lieut. H. Harris	—	May 1916
2/Lieut. R. M. Harris	Killed	June 1917
2/Lieut. J. J. A. Hawtrey	Missing	Sept. 1917
Lieut. J. Headlam	Killed	May 1918
Major J. N. D. Heenan	—	June 1916
Capt. H. G. Hegarty, M.C.. . . .	—	Jan. 1918
Lieut. G. W. Hemsworth	—	Jan. 1918
Lieut. C. R. Henderson	—	March 1918
Lieut. N. P. Henderson	Wounded	April 1917
Capt. E. G. Herbert	Wounded	Jan. 1917
Lieut. H. E. Hervey, M.C. and Bar . .	Missing	April 1917
2/Lieut. F. A. Hickson	—	Sept. 1918
Sqdn.-Ldr. R. M. Hill, M.C., A.F.C. . .	—	Aug. 1916
Capt. C. Holland, M.C.	—	Dec. 1916
2/Lieut. R. Hopper	Killed	Jan. 1917
F/Lieut. S. B. Horn, M.C. . . .	—	Sept. 1917
2/Lieut. E. S. Howard	Killed	May 1917
2/Lieut. G. D. Hunter	Missing	May 1917
2/Lieut. W. E. Jenkins	Killed	Nov. 1917
Lieut. O. P. Johnson.	—	July 1918
Lieut. B. S. Johnston	—	Aug. 1918
Lieut. R. N. K. Jones, M.C. . . .	—	July 1916

Name.	Casualty.	Date.
Lieut. P. S. Joyce	Missing	March 1917
Capt. R. C. Kean	—	Jan. 1917
Capt. G. D. F. Keddie	—	May 1916
Lieut. S. W. Keen, M.C.	Died of Wounds	Aug. 1916
Lieut C. M. Kelly	—	Aug. 1916
2/Lieut. W. M. Kent	Missing	Feb. 1918
Lieut. J. F. M. Kerr	—	Aug. 1918
2/Lieut. J. L. Kight	—	Aug. 1916
2/Lieut. R. E. Kimbell	Missing	April 1917
2/Lieut. C. H. M. King	Killed	Sept. 1916
Capt. A. N. Kingwill.	—	Feb. 1917
Lieut. R. A. Kirkpatrick	—	April 1918
Capt. H. Kirton	—	Jan. 1917
Capt. M. B. Knowles.	Missing	April 1917
Lieut. R. H. Knowles	—	
Lieut. T. Langwill	Missing	April 1917
Capt. J. D. Latta, M.C.	—	Nov. 1916
2/Lieut. J. Laurie-Reid	—	May 1916
Lieut. (Hon. Capt.) J. K. Law . . .	Missing	Sept. 1917
2/Lieut. L. H. Leckie	—	April 1917
Lieut. H. M. Lewis	—	July 1917
Lieut. R. G. Lewis	Missing	March 1918
Lieut. D. R. C. Lloyd	Missing	June 1917
Capt. E. A. Lloyd	—	Jan. 1917
Major G. L. Lloyd, M.C., A.F.C. . .	—	June 1917
Lieut. L. B. Loughran, American Air Service	Killed	July 1918
2/Lieut. J. C. Louw	—	March 1918
Lieut. (Hon. Capt.) R. J. S. Lund . .	—	Sept. 1918
Capt. J. D. McCall	—	Nov. 1917
Lieut. W. F. McCarthy	Wounded	Nov. 1918
Lieut. E. J. C. McCracken . . .	Missing	Aug. 1918
Major J. B. McCudden, V.C., D.S.O. and Bar, M.C. and Bar, Croix de Guerre, Mil. Medal	Killed	July 1918
F/Lieut. B. McEntegart	—	Aug. 1918
Lieut. I. C. MacGregor	Injured	Sept. 1917
2/Lieut. N. C. Mackey	—	Sept. 1918
2/Lieut. C. W. McKissock . . .	Missing	May 1917
2/Lieut. R. D. McLennan	Killed	Dec. 1917
Lieut. J. E. C. MacVicker	Killed	June 1918
2/Lieut. H. E. Martin	Killed	Nov. 1916
F/Officer S. J. Mason	—	Sept. 1918
Major H. Meintjies, M.C., A.F.C. . .	—	May 1916
Capt. P. Middlemas, M.B.E. . . .	—	Feb. 1917
2/Lieut. S. C. Millar	—	July 1918
Major J. A. Milot	Missing	April 1917
Capt. W. E. Molesworth, M.C. and Bar, Italian Medal (Silver) for Military Valour .	—	March 1917
Capt. H. A. S. Molyneux, D.F.C. . .	—	March 1918
Lieut.-Col. B. F. Moore	—	Jan. 1918
Lieut. A. W. Morey, M.C. . . .	Killed	Jan. 1918
Lieut. D. H. Morris	—	Oct. 1917
Capt. F. J. Morse, Croix de Guerre (French)	—	Dec. 1918

Name.	Casualty.	Date.
Lieut. A. W. M. Mowle	Injured	July 1917
Lieut. D. C. G. Murray	Missing	June 1917
2/Lieut. W. B. Newth	Killed	Sept. 1918
2/Lieut. H. J. Newton	Missing	May 1916
Lieut. B. Nicholson	—	Sept. 1917
Lieut. J. I. M. O'Beirne	—	May 1916
Lieut. A. R. Oliver	—	Aug. 1918
Lieut. J. A. N. Ormsby	Missing	July 1916
Lieut. H. C. M. Orpen	—	Sept. 1918
Lieut. E. R. Ortner	—	March 1918
Lieut. F. H. Osborne	—	Sept. 1918
Lieut. G. E. Osmond	—	March 1917
Lieut. C. F. Overy	—	May 1916
Capt. G. A. Parker, M.C., D.S.O. .	Missing	Nov. 1916
Major S. E. Parker, M.B.E., A.F.C. . .	—	Aug. 1916
2/Lieut. F. C. Parkes	—	June 1917
Lieut. G. A. H. Parkes	Missing	July 1917
Capt. C. Parry, D.F.C.	Wounded	July 1918
Major C. K. C. Patrick, D.S.O., M.C. and Bar	—	Aug. 1917
Major C. Patteson, M.C., A.F.C., Croix de Guerre (French) .	—	May 1917
Capt. A. R. Penny, M.C. . . .	—	June 1917
Lieut. E. W. Percival	—	May 1917
2/Lieut. R. M. Phalen	Missing	May 1917
Capt. G. Phillippi, M.C. . . .	Wounded	Sept. 1916
F/Officer G. A. H. Pidcock, Croix de Guerre (French)	—	Jan. 1917
F/Officer S. L. Pope	—	May 1917
Sqdn.-Ldr. C. F. A. Portal, M.C., D.S.O. and Bar	—	May 1916
2/Lieut. O. Price	—	June 1918
Lieut. J. O. Priestley	—	Nov. 1917
Lieut. H. N. J. Proctor	—	March 1918
Capt. E. B. A. Rayner	—	Jan. 1917
Capt. J. W. Rayner	—	Aug. 1918
Lieut. F. K. Read, American Air Service	—	June 1918
F/Lieut. C. A. Ridley, D.S.O., M.C. .	Missing	May 1916
2/Lieut. D. M. Robertson	Missing	April 1917
Lieut. N. McL. Robertson	Killed	Oct. 1916
Lieut. H. G. Ross	Injured	May 1917
Lieut. J. A. Roth, United States Air Service .	—	Oct. 1918
Capt. B. Roxburgh-Smith, D.F.C. and Bar, Croix de Guerre (Belgian) . .	Injured	Feb. 1917
Lieut. N. C. Roystan	Injured	Feb. 1918
Lieut. W. O. Russell	Missing	April 1917
Capt. W. J. Rutherford	—	May 1917
Lieut. A. W. Saunders, D.F.C. . . .	—	Feb. 1918
Capt. O. J. F. Scholte, M.C. . . .	Killed	July 1918
Grp.-Capt. A. J. L. Scott, C.B., M.C., A.F.C. .	Wounded	April 1917
Capt. J. Seabrook, A.F.C. . . .	—	Oct. 1916
Capt. F. H. B. Selous, M.C., Italian Silver Medal	Killed	Sept. 1917
Lieut. W. B. Sherwood	Missing	Oct. 1917
Lieut. R. G. Sillars	—	May 1917

Name.	Casualty.	Date.
F/Lieut. J. H. Simpson	—	May 1916
2/Lieut. M. D. Sinclair	—	June 1918
2/Lieut. G. O. Smart	Missing	April 1917
Sqdn.-Ldr. H. G. Smart	—	May 1916
Lieut. J. E. Smith	Missing	Sept. 1918
2/Lieut. L. H. Smith	Missing	Oct. 1918
Lieut. R. H. Smith	—	Sept. 1918
Lieut.-Col. R. R. Smith-Barry, A.F.C., Chevalier de l'Ordre de Leopold	—	May 1916
F/Lieut. F. O. Soden, D.F.C.	—	July 1917
2/Lieut. L. V. Southwell	Injured	March 1918
Sqdn.-Ldr. W. Sowrey, A.F.C	—	Nov. 1916
Lieut. J. M. J. Spencer	Missing	Oct. 1916
Lieut. F. Stedman	Missing	April 1917
2/Lieut. R. B. Steele	Injured	Sept. 1917
2/Lieut. L. G. Stockwell	Missing	Oct. 1918
T/Capt. V. A. Stookes, M.C.	—	Oct. 1916
2/Lieut. H. S. Stuart-Smith	Missing	Sept. 1918
Lieut. E. A. Sullock, A.F.C.	—	March 1918
Capt. A. S. M. Summers	Missing	Sept. 1916
2/Lieut. H. E. Talbot	—	Dec. 1918
Capt. H. S. Taylor	—	Aug. 1916
Capt. G. J. Temperley	Injured	Oct. 1917
Lieut. G. E. Tennant	—	Sept. 1918
Lieut. O. Thamer	Missing	Jan. 1918
2/Lieut. S. A. Thomson	Missing	Sept. 1918
F/Officer E. Thornton	—	Jan. 1918
Capt. H. C. Tower	Missing	May 1916
F/Lieut. E. J. D. Townesend	Missing	April 1917
Lieut. J. W. Trusler	—	Feb. 1918
2/Lieut. F. E. Upton-Smith	—	Feb. 1918
Capt. S. F. Vincent, A.F.C.	—	July 1916
Lieut. B. M. Wainwright	Missing	July 1916
Major F. F. Waldron	Killed	May 1916
Lieut. Walker	—	Aug. 1916
Lieut. A. M. Walters	—	Sept. 1916
Capt. L. S. Weedon	—	Sept. 1916
2/Lieut. A. N. Westergaard	—	June 1918
2/Lieut. M. West-Thompson	Killed	Sept. 1917
Lieut. A. D. Whitehead	Missing	March 1917
Capt. L. E. Whitehead	Wounded	June 1916
Lieut. J. O. Whiting	Missing	Sept. 1917
Lieut. R. K. Whitney, D.F.C.	Wounded	Aug. 1918
2/Lieut. R. C. R. Wilde	—	Oct. 1918
Lieut. C. Williams	Missing	May 1916
2/Lieut. V. F. Williams	Missing	April 1917
2/Lieut. J. Winslow	—	Oct. 1918
Lieut. C. O. Wright	—	Aug. 1917
Lieut. G. C. Young	—	May 1917

APPENDIX II

BATTLE CASUALTIES

In this list each officer is given in the rank which he held at the time he was wounded or missing. It is very apparent that it was during April 1917 that the squadron went through the bitterest fighting. There were 20 casualties in this month alone. The worst month after this was September 1917, with 8 casualties, while in July and again in September 1918, 6 pilots " went west."

These figures show clearly the increase in the intensity of air fighting as the contest wore on. In August 1916, when 60 was still a two-seater squadron with only one scout flight, we lost 5 pilots and 2 observers ; this was thought at the time to be high, as indeed it was according to the standard of those days, though several other squadrons lost more heavily during the Somme. Nevertheless, the figures show only too clearly that the Arras fighting was far the severest trial 60 ever had, for during April 1917 the losses were 105 per cent. The total number of Battle Casualties is 115, sustained during 29 months of war flying, giving an average of just under 4 per month, or nearly one a week.

An analysis of the figures shows that 76 of these 115 were killed, while 39 are alive, unless, indeed, they were killed with another squadron later in the war : but this could only have happened to the 21 wounded who got back to their own side of the lines.

Of the 72 missing, 54 are dead, 17 were repatriated from Germany, while one, Ridley, escaped.

Though it was true to say that roughly half of our missing in the Air Force were alive, it will be seen that in 60's case the average was much smaller, only 25 per cent. instead of 50 per cent.

Name.	Casualty.	Date.	Details.
Major F. F. Waldron	Killed	3.7.16	Died whilst Prisoner of War.
Lieut. N. A. Browning-Paterson	Missing	21.7.16	Officially reported killed.
Lieut. L. E. Whitehead	Wounded	30.7.16	(Missing 20.5.18—65 Sqdn.) Death presumed.
Lieut. W. E. G. Bryant	Wounded	30.7.16	
Capt. L. S. Charles	Missing	30.7.16	Died whilst P. of W.
Lieut. C. Williams	Killed	30.7.16	
2/Lieut. L. L. Clark	Missing	2.8.16	Death accepted.
Lieut. J. A. N. Ormsby	Missing	2.8.16	Officially reported killed.
2/Lieut. H. J. Newton	Missing	2.8.16	Death accepted 2.8.16.
F/Lieut. C. A. Ridley	Missing	3.8.16	Escaped from Germany 13.10.16.
2/Lieut. J. M. Drysdale	Wounded	25.8.16	
2/Lieut. B. M. Wainwright	Missing	28.8.16	Repatriated P. of W. 1.1.19.
Capt. A. S. M. Summers	Missing	15.9.16	Killed.
Capt. H. C. Tower	Missing	19.9.16	Death accepted.
2/Lieut. G. Phillippi	Wounded	26.9.16	
Lieut. N. McL. Robertson	Killed	17.10.16	Died of wounds.
2260 Sergt. A. Walker	Killed	25.10.16	
Lieut. W. M. Carlyle	Missing	26.10.16	Death accepted.
Lieut. J. M. J. Spencer	Missing	3.11.16	Killed.
Lieut. A. D. Bell-Irving	Wounded	9.11.16	
2/Lieut. H. E. Martin	Killed	16.11.16	
Lieut. D. H. Bacon	Missing	16.11.16	Death accepted.
Capt. G. A. Parker	Missing	27.11.16	Death accepted.
Capt. E. D. Grenfell	Wounded	11.12.16	
2/Lieut. E. J. L. W. Gilchrist	Wounded	11.12.16	
2/Lieut. R. Hopper	Killed	11.1.17	Savy.
2/Lieut. E. G. Herbert	Wounded	28.1.17	While salving a wrecked [machine.
Major E. P. Graves	Killed	6.3.17	Rivière.
2/Lieut. P. S. Joyce	Missing	6.3.17	
Lieut. A. D. Whitehead	Missing	11.3.17	Repatriated P. of W. 20.1.18.
Lieut. C. McH. M. Caffyn	Killed	28.3.17	Le Hameau.
Lieut. W. P. Garnett	Missing	30.3.17	Death accepted.
2/Lieut. F. Bower	Died of wounds	31.3.17	Died of wounds.
2/Lieut. V. F. Williams	Missing	2.4.17	Death accepted.
Lieut. E. J. D. Townesend	Missing	5.4.17	Repatriated P. of W. 20.1.18.

Name.	Casualty.	Date.	Details.
2/Lieut. G. O. Smart	Missing	7.4.17	Killed.
2/Lieut. C. S. Hall .	Missing	7.4.17	Killed.
Capt. M. B. Knowles	Missing	7.4.17	Repatriated P. of W 14.12.18.
Lieut. W. O. Russell .	Missing	14.4.17	Repatriated P. of W. 2.1.19.
2/Lieut. L. C. Chapman	Missing	14.4.17	Died of wounds.
Capt. A. Binnie .	Missing	14.4.17	Repatriated P. of W 7.1.18.
2/Lieut. J. H. Cock .	Missing	14.4.17	Death accepted.
2/Lieut. H. E. Hervey	Missing	15.4.17	Repatriated P. of W.
Major J. A. Milot .	Missing	15.4.17	Reported dead (German source).
Lieut. J. McC. Elliott	Killed	16.4.17	
2/Lieut. D. N. Robertson . . .	Missing	16.4.17	Death accepted.
Lieut. T. Langwill .	Missing	16.4.17	Death accepted.
2/Lieut. R. E. Kimbell . . .	Missing	16.4.17	Killed in action.
Lieut. T. L. Atkinson	Wounded	20.4.17	
2/Lieut. N. P. Henderson . . .	Wounded	26.4.17	
2/Lieut. F. Stedman	Missing	27.4.17	Repatriated P. of W. 31.12.18.
2/Lieut. H. G. Ross .	Wounded	28.4.17	
2/Lieut. R. B. Clark	Died of wounds	30.4.17	Died of wounds 1.5.17.
2/Lieut. C. W. McKissock . .	Missing	6.5.17	Repatriated P. of W. 14.12.18.
Lieut. G. D Hunter	Missing	6.5.17	Repatriated P. of W. 20.1.18.
2/Lieut. E. S. Howard	Killed	18.5.17	Tilloy-les-Hemaville.
2/Lieut. R. J. Grandin	Killed	18.5.17	N. Rémy.
2/Lieut. W. Gilchrist	Missing	25.5.17	Repatriated P. of W. 17.11.18.
2/Lieut. R. M. Phalen	Missing	28.5.17	Killed.
2/Lieut. R. M. Harris	Killed	7.6.17	Le Hameau.
Lieut. D. R. C. Lloyd	Missing	16.6.17	Reported dead (German source).
Lieut. D. C. G. Murray	Missing	27.6.17	Repatriated P. of W 9.12.18.
Lieut. A. R. Adam .	Missing	3.7.17	Killed.
Major A. J. L. Scott.	Wounded	10.7.17	
2/Lieut. G. A. H. Parkes . .	Missing	15.7.17	Repatriated P. of W 23.12.18.
Lieut. A. W. M. Mowle	Wounded	22.7.17	
2/Lieut. W. H. Gunner	Missing	29.7.17	Death accepted.
Lieut. H. T. Hammond	Missing	14.9.17	Repatriated P. of W 18.12.18.
2/Lieut. J. J. A. Hawtrey . .	Missing	16.9.17	Reported died (German source).
19130 Sergt. J. W. Bancroft . .	Missing	20.9.17	Repatriated P of W 19.12.18.

Name.	Casualty.	Date.	Details.
Capt. J. K. Law .	Missing	21.9.17	Death accepted.
Lieut. J. O. Whiting	Missing	22.9.17	Death accepted.
Lieut. I. C. MacGregor	Wounded	22.9.17	
89279 2/A.M. H. H. Bright . .	Missing	23.9.17	Reported killed 19.10.17.
2/Lieut. J. H. Flynn.	Killed	30.9.17	
2/Lieut. J. J. Fitzgerald	Missing	5.10.17	Repatriated P of W. 18.12.18.
Lieut. W. B. Sherwood	Missing	27.10.17	Death accepted.
Capt. J. C. A. Caunter	Missing	28.10.17	Killed.
Lieut. W. E. Jenkins	Killed	23.11.17	
2/Lieut. M. West-Thompson . .	Killed	23.11.17	
2/Lieut. R. W. McLennan . .	Killed	23.12.17	
Capt. F. H. B. Selous	Killed	4.1.18	Collision in the air.
2/Lieut. O. Thamer .	Missing	6.1.18	Repatriated P. of W 22.11.18.
Lieut. A. W. Morey, M.C. . . .	Killed	24.1.18	
2/Lieut. A. C. Ball .	Missing	5.2.18	Repatriated P of W. 14.12.18.
2/Lieut. N. C. Roystan	Wounded	18.2.18	
2/Lieut. C. B. Craig .	Missing	21.2.18	Death accepted.
2/Lieut. W. M. Kent	Missing	21.2.18	Death accepted.
Lieut. L. V. Southwell	Wounded	6.3.18	Died of wounds 14.3.18.
2/Lieut. E. W. Christie	Missing	2.4.18	Presumed dead.
Capt. K. Crawford .	Missing	11.4.18	Presumed dead.
2/Lieut. H. N. J. Proctor . .	Missing	16.5.18	Presumed dead.
Lieut. J. Headlam .	Killed	30.5.18	
Capt. J. D. Belgrave	Missing	13.6.18	Presumed dead.
Lieut. R. G. Lewis .	Missing	13.6.18	Repatriated P of W. 13.12.18.
Lieut. H. A. Gordon	Missing	7.7.18	Presumed dead.
Capt. G. C. Dell-Clarke	Killed	16.7.18	
Lieut. J. S. Griffith .	Wounded	18.7.18	
Lieut. J. E. C. Mac-Vicker . .	Missing	22.7.18	Presumed dead.
Lieut. L. B. Loughram	Killed	28.7.18	
Capt. C. Parry . .	Wounded	29.7.18	Wounded.
2/Lieut. J. G. Hall .	Missing	8.8.18	Presumed dead.
2/Lieut. H. Buckley .	Wounded	10.8.18	
2/Lieut. R. K. Whitney	Wounded	11.8.18	
Lieut. J. R. Anderson	Killed	13.8.18	
Lieut. E. C. J. Mc-Cracken . .	Missing	13.8.18	Repatriated P. of W 14.12.18.
Lieut. S. W. Keen .	Killed	21.8.18	Died of wounds at 3rd Can. C.C.S.
2/Lieut. S. A. Thomson	Missing	5.9.18	Presumed dead.
Capt. J. E. Doyle .	Missing	5.9.18	Repatriated P. of W 30.12.18.
Lieut. J. E. Smith .	Missing	17.9.18	Reported killed in action
2/Lieut. H. S. Smith.	Missing	15.9.18	Killed in action.

Name.	Casualty.	Date.	Details.
Lieut. G. F. C. Caswell	Missing	20.9.18	Repatriated P. of W. 9.12.18.
2/Lieut. H. F. V. Battle	Wounded	20.9.18	
Lieut. L. H. Smith .	Missing	26.10.18	Repatriated P. of W. 9.12.18.
2/Lieut. L. G. Stockwell . . .	Missing	28.10.18	Repatriated P. of W. 9.12.18.

APPENDIX III

COMBAT CLAIMS
MADE BY MEMBERS OF SIXTY SQUADRON
1916–1918

1. This listing has been compiled after much sifting of evidence available from many, frequently contradictory, sources. Many of the claims shown have never been substantiated, but are meritorious, whereas some vague claims of enemy aircraft driven down have not been included. Public Record Office references between them do not include a complete set of all submitted, serially-numbered, combat claims. Errors and omissions in the Officers Record Books (which were recommenced late in November, 1916, after the fire in the Squadron Office), do not match the logbooks of the individual pilots contacted, or with consolidated returns/summaries by successive Sqn. Cdrs. and those in higher posts, when recommendations for awards were written. Some further evidence has come to light subsequently but this listing can only be considered non-conclusive, and always subject to amendment. However, it has been quite obvious, for over six decades, that solo, unwitnessed, claims made by the odd survivor of WW1 have no substantiation in German records.

   The numbers quoted after the Sqn. pilot's names indicate claims made in sequence, and where known, indicate success with earlier Sqns. However, in 1918, these begin to reflect acknowledged/substantiated claims. If only the records had been equally discriminatory in 1917, much of the heated controversy from the mid-1920s onwards may have been avoided!

The names quoted in parentheses as likely German victims are on advice from many sources, but are frequently conjectural as attempting to match date, time, place, combat details and aircraft types between the various records available.

2. 60 Sqn. casualties known to have been incurred in particular combats are shown. There were many other casualties in combat when no claim was made, but such are listed elsewhere.

3. As air fighting developed during World War 1, some changes occurred in the terminology used and the requirements for substantiation of claims. For the purpose of this listing, the following terms are used throughout:

DD: Driven Down, i.e. forced to break off and flee under control

DOOC: Sent down out of control, but not seen to crash

FTL: Forced to Land, i.e. seen to alight, but not crash, after combat, usually due to damage or wounds inflicted

Crashed: Enemy aircraft seen to hit the ground after combat and presumed written off

Destroyed: Enemy aircraft broke up in the air as the result of combat

Flamer: Enemy aircraft set on fire and presumed destroyed

4. Abbreviations used in this and other Appendices are:

OP Offensive Patrol   DP Defensive Patrol
COP Close OP   DOP Distant OP
KIA Killed in Action   WIA Wounded in
POW Prisoner of War   Action

DOI Died of Injuries sustained in accident
DOW Died of Wounds sustained in action
E/A Enemy Aircraft
2s Unidentified two-seater
F/L Forced Landing not due to enemy action
Le P Le Prieur rockets
KB Kite Balloon
B/O Baled or jumped out, i.e. with or without parachute respectively

5. OP victories are primarily credited to the patrol leader as his skill and tactics were usually responsible for the engagement, and he was normally the first to fire. If the names of other patrol members also firing at the victim are known, they are credited with a share of the victory.

6. Contemporary comments on scores achieved by individuals and the Sqn. are shown in chronological sequence. (Exceptionally, some claims are cumulative, whereas all others entirely reflect 60 Sqn. claims: such differences are minor overall, but previous service in other units with a fighter/scout capability should be considered: Ball, Latta, Goodrich, Foot, etc.)

7. Times quoted are Allied standard times. In 1915, the Germans introduced Summer Time (A to B) as a fuel-saving measure, and in May, 1916, Britain followed suit (Z to A). Thus German standard time on the Western Front was usually one hour ahead except when the change from/to Summer Time did not coincide, i.e. times were synchronised during the following periods:

25/3/17 to 16/4/17; 10/3/18 to 15/4/18; 16/9/18 to 6/10/18

D. W. Warne
1990

DATE	AIRCREW	AIRCRAFT/SERIAL	ENEMY AIRCRAFT	CLAIM	PLACE	TIME
1/7/16	Maj. Waldron & OP	Bullets	LVG	FTL	Bapaume	11.45
2/7/16	Lts. B-Paterson/Bryant (Obs. WIA) 60 crew FTL	Biplane	LVG	DD		
2/7/16	Lts. Whitehead/Clark OP	Biplane	Fokker EIII	DOOC	German Lines	
2/7/16			?	FTL		
11/7/16	Capt. Tower	Bullet	?	DD?	Bois d'Havrincourt	am
11/7/16	Lt. Meintjes	Bullet	?	DD?	Bois d'Havrincourt	am
19/7/16	2 Lt. Ridley	Bullet	Fokker	Flamer?		
21/7/16	Capt. Summers Le P	Biplane	KB	?		
27/7/16	2 Lt. Vincent	Bullet	LVG	Crashed	15 E of line	18.00+
27/7/16	2 Lt. Smart	Bullet	LVG?	FTL	in lines	18.00+
27/7/16	2 Lt. Wainwright	Bullet A167	LVG	DD	in lines	
28/7/16	Capt. Tower (2) OP	Bullet	LVG	FTL		16.00+
30/7/16		Biplane	?	Crashed?		
	(Sqn. score: 4 confirmed)					
	3/8/16, Sqn. withdrawn to re-equip and re-train until 23/8/16					
24/8/16	Capt. Tower (3)	Bullet A204	LVG?	DD	Bois d'Adinfer	10.45
25/8/16	2 Lt. Smart (2)	Bullet A202	Roland	DD	Bapaume	09.25
25/8/16	2 Lt. Wainwright (2)	Bullet A179	Roland C	DOOC?	S. Arras	11.00
25/8/16	2 Lt. Ball (12)	Nieuport A201	Roland CII	DOOC	Bapaume	09.15
25/8/16	2 Lt. Ball (13)	Nieuport A201	Roland CII	DOOC	Bapaume	to
25/8/16	2 Lt. Ball (14)	Nieuport A201	Roland CII	Crashed	Bapaume	09.30
25/8/16	2 Lt. Ball (15)	Nieuport A201	Roland CII	FTL	Le Transloy	09.30
28/8/16	(von Arnim KIA) Lt. Bell-Irving Wainwright FTL, POW	Bullet A166	Roland CII	Crashed	Bapaume	18.40
28/8/16	2 Lt. Walters	Nieuport A164	LVG C	DOOC	10 E of Somme	19.00
28/8/16	2 Lt. Ball (16)	Nieuport A201	Roland CII/LVG C	FTL	Grevillers	19.00
28/8/16	2 Lt. Ball (17)	Nieuport A201	Roland CII	FTL	Beugny	19.00+
28/8/16	2 Lt. Ball (18)	Nieuport A201	Roland CII	Crashed	E Ayette	19.00
28/8/16	2 Lt. Ball	Nieuport A201	C	DD	?	19.00
	(30/8/16: Ball credited with 11 crashed, 5 DOOC, 12 FTL/Damaged, 1+ KB)					
31/8/16	Capt. Summers	Bullet A179	LVG C	DD	Bapaume	10.00
31/8/16	Capt. Goodrich	Nieuport A200	LVG C	DOOC	Vaux Wood	11.45
31/8/16	Lt. Latta	Nieuport A135	LVG C	DOOC	Bapaume	18.45

DATE	AIRCREW	AIRCRAFT/SERIAL	ENEMY AIRCRAFT	CLAIM	PLACE	TIME
31/8/16	2 Lt. Ball (19)	Nieuport A201	Roland CII	Crashed	SE Cambrai	
31/8/16	2 Lt. Ball (20)	Nieuport A201	Roland CII	FTL	SE Bapaume	
These two claims were made between 18.30–20.20 after which Ball was FTL. (31/8/16: Ball credited with 20 official victories; 8 confirmed,						
12 unconfirmed, 2 KB destroyed + 1 unconfirmed)						
3/9/16	2 Lt. Joyce (Pilot KIA)	Bullet A198	AGO C-II?	Crashed	Noreuil	11.00
No combat activity for about a week						
14/9/16	Lt. Bell-Irving (2)	Nieuport A203	KB	Destroyed	Avesnes les B.	18.45
15/9/16	2 Lt. Gilchrist	Nieuport A201	KB	Destroyed	Bapaume	09.00
15/9/16	Capt. Summers (3)	Nieuport A136	KB	Destroyed	Bapaume	09.00
All three of the above KB attacks were with Le P rockets.						
Capt. Summers KIA on this sortie.						
15/9/16	2 Lt. Walters (2)	Nieuport A164	LVG C	Flamer	S. Bapaume	09.15
15/9/16	2 Lts. Hill/Carlyle	Bullets A179/5196	Roland C	DD	Bapaume	09.20
15/9/16	2 Lt. Cole	Bullets A174	Roland C	DOOC	Bapaume	09.45
15/9/16	Lt. Ball (21)	Nieuport A200	DII	Crashed	Beugny	09.55
15/9/16	Lt. Ball (22) (von Wurmb WIA)	Nieuport A212	Albatros CIII	FTL	Nurlu	15.00
15/9/16	Lt. Ball (23) (du Cornu/Carstens DOW/WIA)	Nieuport A201	Roland CII	Crashed	NE Bertincourt	19.50
17/9/16	2 Lt. Philippi	Nieuport A187	LVG C	DD	Adinfer Wood	08.05
19/9/16	Lt. Ball (24)	Nieuport A213	Albatros A	FTL	S St. Leger	18.15
19/9/16	Capt. Tower (4) Tower KIA	Bullet A204	Fokker DIII	Collision	Grevillers	18.30?
19/9/16	Lt. Latta (2)	Nieuport A135	D	DOOC	Achiet le Grand	18.30
21/9/16	Lt. Ball (25)	Nieuport A213	Roland D	FTL	Bapaume	15.30+
21/9/16	Lt. Ball (26)	Nieuport A213	Roland D	Crashed	St. Leger	16.30–
21/9/16	Lt. Ball (27)	Nieuport A213	Roland CII	Crashed	Bucquoy	17.15–18.30
21/9/16	Lt. Philippi (2)	Nieuport A201	LVG?	DOOC	Bapaume	18.20
22/9/16	2 Lt. Smart (3) (Magercurth KIA?)	Bullet A202	LVG C	DD	Bapaume	11.00
22/9/16	2 Lt. Walters (3) (Abert KIA?)	Nieuport A164	Albatros? D	DD	SE Bapaume	11.30
22/9/16	Lt. Ball (28) shared with FE2b of 11 Sqn. (Kohn/Reichel KIA Bertincourt)	Nieuport A213	Roland CII	FTL	SE Bapaume	11.30
22/9/16	Lt. Ball (29) (Grafe KIA)	Nieuport A213	Fokker D	Crashed	E Bapaume	17.00

DATE	AIRCREW	AIRCRAFT/SERIAL	ENEMY AIRCRAFT	CLAIM	PLACE	TIME
23/9/16	Lt. Bell-Irving (3)	Nieuport A203	Roland CII?	Crashed	Croisilles	12.30
23/9/16	Lt. Ball (30)	Nieuport A213	Albatros C	Flamer	Mory	18.00+
	Ball FTL					
25/9/16	Capt. Ball (31)	Nieuport A213	Albatros A	Crashed	Bapaume-Cambrai	18.30
	(Tewes/Hoffman WIA/KIA)					
26/9/16	2 Lt. Hill (2)	Nieuport A212	KB	Flamer	Boisleux	11.20
	Le P					
26/9/16	Lt. Philippi (3)	Nieuport A201	KB	Flamer	Bapaume	11.30
	Le P					
	Philippi WIA					
26/9/16	Capt. Ball (32)	Nieuport A213	Roland CII/Albatros A	DD	Sapignies	18.00
	(Obs. WIA)					
28/9/16	Capt. Ball (33)	Nieuport A213	Albatros C	Crashed	Haplincourt	17.45
28/9/16	Capt. Ball (34)	Nieuport A213	Roland CII/Albatros A	FTL	Bapaume	18.30
	(Schedler WIA)					
28/9/16	Capt. Ball (35)	Nieuport A213	Roland CII/Albatros C	FTL	Haplincourt	18.30+
28/9/16	Capt. Foot (3)	SPAD A253	Albatros C	Crashed	Avesnes les B.	18.10+
30/9/16	Lt. Bell-Irving (4)	Nieuport A203	Roland C	Crashed	Villers au Flos	10.40
30/9/16	Lt. Bell-Irving (5)	Nieuport A203	Roland C	Flamer?	Villers au Flos	10.40+
30/9/16	2 Lt. Vincent (2)	Nieuport A215	Roland C	Flamer	Villers au Flos	10.45
30/9/16	Capt. Ball (36)	Nieuport A201	Albatros A	Flamer	Velu	10.55
	(+ 11 Sqn.) (Obs. B/O)					
30/9/16	Lt. Walters (4)	Nieuport A164	Albatros D?	DD	Bapaume	10.45
	(Diener KIA?)					
30/9/16	Capt. Ball (37)	Nieuport A213	Roland CII	DOOC	Graincourt	18.37
30/9/16	Capt. Ball	Nieuport A213	?	DOOC?	Graincourt	18.39
1/10/16	Capt. Ball (38)	Nieuport A213	Albatros D	FTL	Gommecourt	07.20
	(Phillips KIA at Bapaume?)					
1/10/16	Capt. Ball (39)	Nieuport A213	Albatros A	FTL	Hamelincourt	07.35
1/10/16	Capt. Ball (40)	Nieuport A213	Albatros A	FTL	Hamelincourt	08.25
(On completion of his tour in France, Capt. Ball was credited with: 16 crashed, 5 DOOC, 18 FTL, 8 DD: KBs 1 destroyed and 2 DD.)						
No Sqn. combat activity for about 2 weeks.						
15/10/16	Lt. Bell-Irving (6)	Nieuport A203	C	Crashed	Ervillers	12.00+
15/10/16	Lt. Bell-Irving (7)	Nieuport A203	C	DOOC	Ervillers	12.00+
20/10/16	Capt. Grenfell	Nieuport A208	Albatros D	DOOC	Rocquigny	10.15
20/10/16	Capt. Grenfell & OP	Nieuport A208/+	Albatros C	DOOC/DD?	E. Bapaume	10.35
20/10/16	2 Lt. Gilchrist (2)	Nieuport A235?	LVG C	DOOC	Gommecourt	10.40

DATE	AIRCREW	AIRCRAFT/SERIAL	ENEMY AIRCRAFT	CLAIM	PLACE	TIME
20/10/16	Capt. Foot (4) (+ DH2S.) (Obs. W1A?)	Nieuport A212	Albatros A	DD	Bapaume	16.15
21/10/16	Capt. Foot (5)	Nieuport A212	Roland C	DOOC	Biencourt	16.00
21/10/16	Lt. Meintjes (& 1)	Nieuport ?	LVG	DD	SE Bapaume	16.25
21/10/16	2 Lt. Pidcock	Nieuport A125	Albatros C	DD	Bapaume	08.15
22/10/16	Lt. Meintjes	Nieuport A214	Roland C	DOOC	Bapaume	16.10
2/11/16	2 Lt. Joyce	Nieuport A224	KB	Smoking	Arras	pm
3/11/16	Lt. Spencer Spencer WIA, POW. (Koenig WIA)	Nieuport A125	Albatros DI?	DOOC	Douchy	
9/11/16	Capt. Bell-Irving (9) Bell-Irving WIA	Nieuport A272	Halberstadt C	DD	Le Transloy	09.30
9/11/16	2 Lt. Gilchrist (Obs. jumped)	Nieuport ?	Roland C	Flamer	Le Transloy	09.30
9/11/16	2 Lt. Hill (5)	Nieuport A271	Roland DI	DD	Bapaume	09.30
9/11/16	2 Lt. Armstrong A211 damaged	Nieuport A211	Roland DI	DD	Havrincourt	10.00
9/11/16	Lt. Meintjes (3) Poor weather for about 3 weeks.	Nieuport A274	LVG	FTL	Lagnicourt	15.15
19/11/16	2 Lt. Caldwell (Obs. WIA)	Nieuport A279	LVG?	DD		
28/11/16	Capt. Sowrey/ Lts. Pidcock/Seabrook	Nieuports A271/A214/A208	KB	DD		11.00
11/12/16	Capt. Grenfell/Lt. Meintjes Grenfell IIA. (174/16=G1 Pilot POW, DOW. Obs. Baldamus DOI)	Nieuports A278/A274	Albatros CIII	FTL	Dainville	10.30
20/12/16	2 Lt. Vincent (3)	Nieuport A215	LVG?	DD	Arras	12.00
20/12/16	Capt. Hill (4)	Nieuport A306	? D	DOOC	Roeux	14.00
27/12/16	Capt. Sowrey/Lts. Pidcock/Giles (+29 Sqn.) Poor weather for about a month.	Nieuports A307/A208/A201	Roland DI	DD	Ficheux	15.25
23/1/17	Capt. Meintjes (5)	Nieuport A311	Rumpler C	DD	Bois d'Adinfer	11.00
23/1/17	Capt. Meintjes (6)	Nieuport A311	Rumpler C	DD	Bois d'Adinfer	15.00
24/1/17	2 Lt. Vincent (4)	Nieuport A6645	Albatros CV?	Crashed	Doullens-Monchy	10.40
27/1/17	Capt. Meintjes (7)	Nieuport A311	Albatros C	DD	Gommecourt	10.45+
27/1/17	Capt. Meintjes (8) Caldwell FTL	Nieuport A311	Albatros C	DD	Gommecourt	10.45+
27/1/17	Capt. Meintjes/Lt. Weedon	Nieuports A279/A214	Albatros C	FTL	Bois de Biez	13.45

DATE	AIRCREW	AIRCRAFT/SERIAL	ENEMY AIRCRAFT	CLAIM	PLACE	TIME
27/1/17	Capt. Meintjes/Lt. Fry	Nieuports A279/A274	Albatros C	FTL	Gommecourt	14.00
29/1/17	Capt. Meintjes (11)	Nieuport A311	Albatros D	Destroyed	Bois de Biez	10.30
29/1/17	Capt. Meintjes/Lts. Fry/Caldwell Caldwell FTL	Nieuports A311/A274/A279	Albatros D	DD	Bois de Biez	10.30+
29/1/17	Capt. Meintjes (13)	Nieuports A311	Albatros C	Crashed	Bois de Biez	10.30+
	Poor weather for about a week					
7/2/17	Capt. Meintjes (14)	Nieuport A311	LVG	DD	Gommecourt	13.00
14/2/17	Lts. Stookes/Giles/Williams	Nieuports A6647/A311/A6645	?C	DOOC	Souastre	12.40
	(Lt. Vincent: 3 confirmed, 3 unconfirmed)					
11/3/17	Lt. Whitehead	Nieuport A279	?D	DOOC	NE Arras	11.00
	Whitehead, WIA, POW					
	Poor weather for about a month					
17/3/17	Maj. Scott/Lt. Molesworth	Nieuports A306/A200	Biplane	DD	NE Arras	10.45
25/3/17	Lt. Bishop	Nieuport A306	Albatros DIII	Crashed	N St. Leger	17.00
	(G15? Pilot KIA?)					
25/3/17	2 Lt. Binnie	Nieuport A6772	Albatros DIII	Crashed	Mercatel	17.00
	(G16? Pilot POW)					
25/3/17	2 Lt. Bower	Nieuport A311	Albatros DIII	DOOC smoking	Mercatel	17.00
31/3/17	Maj. Scott/Capt. Black	Nieuports A6647/A6770	Albatros DIII	Crashed	Heninel	07.30
31/3/17	Lt. Bishop (2)	Nieuport A6769	Albatros DIII	Crashed	S Gavrelle	07.30
31/3/17	Lts. Molesworth/Binnie	Nieuports A6763/A6772	Rumpler C	FTL	S Queant	08.15
31/3/17	2 Lt. Binnie (3)	Nieuport A6772	Albatros D?	DD	E Roclincourt	08.55
31/3/17	Lt. Townesend	Nieuport A6693	Albatros D?	DD	Arras	pm
2/4/17	2 Lt. Hall	Nieuport A6766	Albatros D	DOOC	Fontaine	07.45
	Williams KIA. (Koenig & Wortmann KIA (Vitry))					
5/4/17	2 Lts. Pidcock/Langwill/ Robertson	Nieuports A6770/A6772/A311	Albatros D	DOOC	Riencourt	18.45
6/4/17	Lt. Bishop (Eicholz & Hoppe KIA)	Nieuport A6769	Albatros DIII	DD	Cherisy	09.35
7/4/17	2 Lt. Hall or G. Smart Hall and Smart KIA, Robertson WIA.	Nieuport A6766 or A6645	Albatros D	Crashed	Arras	17.00+
7/4/17	Lt. Bishop (3)	Nieuport A6769	Albatros DIII	DOOC	Arras	17.00
7/4/17	Lt. Bishop	Nieuport A6769	KB	Smoking	Vis-en-Artois	17.10
8/4/17	Maj. Scott/Lt. Bishop	Nieuports A6647/A6769	Albatros CV	Crashed	Douai-Fouquieres	09.30
8/4/17	Lt. Bishop	Nieuport A6769	KB	DD	Arras	09.30+

DATE	AIRCREW	AIRCRAFT/SERIAL	ENEMY AIRCRAFT	CLAIM	PLACE	TIME
8/4/17	Lt. Bishop (4)	Nieuport A6769	Albatros DIII	DOOC	NE Arras	09.40
8/4/17	Lt. Bishop (5)	Nieuport A6769	AEG CIV?	DD	E Arras	09.40+
8/4/17	Lt. Bishop (6)	Nieuport A6769	Albatros DIII	Destroyed	Vitry-en-Artois	10.10
	Milot KIA, Hervey POW. (Frankl KIA) (Capt. Binnie: 3 destroyed, KB attacked)					
13/4/17	Maj. Scott (4) (Obs. WIA?)	Nieuport A6647	Albatros C	FTL	Plouvain	07.20
14/4/17	Capt. Binnie	Nieuport A6772	Albatros D	DOOC	Roclincourt	08.30
14/4/17	Capt. Binnie (Bierling KIA?)	Nieuport A6772	Albatros D	DOOC	Lens	09.15+
14/4/17	Capt. Binnie	Nieuport A6772	2s	DD	Lens	09.15+
14/4/17	Capt. Binnie	Nieuport A6772	2s	DD	Lens	09.15+
	Binnie WIA, FTL, POW; Russell FTL, POW; Cock KIA; Chapman FTL, POW, DOW					
16/4/17	2 Lt. Pidcock	Nieuport A6770	Albatros D	DD	Plouvain-Rouex	09.15
16/4/17	2 Lt. Pidcock (Festner FTL?)	Nieuport A6770	Albatros D	DD	Plouvain	09.15+
	Elliott, Kimbell, Robertson KIA; Langwill FTL, POW, DOW Squadron re-training and poor weather for a few days					
20/4/17	Lt. Bishop (7) (Schaefer? – uninjured)	Nieuport B1566	Aviatik C	Flamer	Biache-St. Vaast	14.58
22/4/17	Lt. Molesworth (Obs. B/O)	Nieuport B1569	KB	Smoking	Vis-en-Artois	07.05
22/4/17	2 Lt. Ross (Two B/O)	Nieuport B1512	KB	Flamer	N Dury	07.05
22/4/17	2 Lt. G. L. Lloyd (Two B/O)	Nieuport B6776	KB	Destroyed	NE Boiry-Notre Dame	07.05
22/4/17	Lt. Patteson	Nieuport B1514	KB	DD	Vis-en-Artois	07.10
22/4/17	2 Lt. Penny	Nieuport B1503	KB	Destroyed		07.30
22/4/17	Lt. Bishop (8)	Nieuport B1566	Albatros DIII	DOOC	Vis-en-Artois	11.20
22/4/17	Lt. Bishop	Nieuport B1566	Fokker D	DD	Vis-en-Artois	11.21
22/4/17	Lt. Patteson	Nieuport B1514	Albatros D	Crashed	Vitry	17.20
22/4/17	Lt. Molesworth (4)	Nieuport B1569	Albatros D	DOOC	Vitry	17.20
22/4/17	Maj. Scott & OP	Nieuport B1575	Albatros CV?	DD	Biache-St. Vaast	18.00
22/4/17	Maj. Scott	Nieuport B1575	Albatros D	DD	Biache-St. Vaast	18.45
23/4/17	Lt. Bishop (10) (crew WIA?)	Nieuport B1566	Albatros CIII	FTL	Vitry-en-Art	15.30

DATE	AIRCREW	AIRCRAFT/SERIAL	ENEMY AIRCRAFT	CLAIM	PLACE	TIME
23/4/17	Lt. Bishop (11)	Nieuport B1566	Albatros DIII	Destroyed?	E Vitry	15.49
	(S. Festner KIA Gavrelle 15.59?)					
24/4/17	2 Lt. Clark	Nieuport A6777	2s	Damaged	E Arras	10.30
	(Obs. WIA?)					
24/4/17	2 Lt. Clark	Nieuport A6777	Albatros D	Crashed?	S Tilloy	13.00
	Clark WIA, FTL, DOW					
24/4/17	Lt. Molesworth (5)	Nieuport B1569	KB	Flamer	Boiry-Notre Dame	13.05
27/4/17	Lt. Bishop	Nieuport B1566	KB	Smoking	Vitry-en-Artois	08.55
29/4/17	Capt. Bishop (12)	Nieuport B1566	Halberstadt DIII	Flamer	E Epinoy	11.55
30/4/17	Capt. Bishop (13)	Nieuport B1566	Albatros? CIII	Crashed	SE Lens	11.15
	(Rodenbeck WIA?)					
30/4/17	Capt. Bishop	Nieuport B1566	Albatros C	FTL	Wancourt-S Lens	11.15+
30/4/17	Capt. Bishop	Nieuport B1566	Albatros CIII	FTL	Monchy-S Lens	12.08
	(35 victories claimed in April 1917, including KBs)					
2/5/17	Lt. Fry (3)	Nieuport B1597	Albatros D	FTL?	Drocourt-Vitry	10.00
2/5/17	Capt. Bishop (15)	Nieuport B1566	Albatros CIII	Crashed?	E Epinoy	10.10
	(Caastel KIA, Weinschenk WIA)					
2/5/17	Capt. Bishop (16)	Nieuport B1566	Albatros CIII	DOOC	E Lens	10.12
2/5/17	Capt. Bishop	Nieuport B1566	2s	DD	Drocourt	12.20
2/5/17	Lt. Fry (4)	Nieuport B1503	Albatros D	DOOC	Vitry-Belonne	15.45
2/5/17	Lt. Horn	Nieuport B1539	2s	Crashed	SW Eterpigny	16.30
2/5/17	Maj. Scott (7)	Nieuport B1575	Albatros	Crashed	Brebieres-Vitry	16.30
4/5/17	Capt. Bishop/Lt. Fry	Nieuports B1566/B1597	AEG CV	Crashed	Cambrai	13.30
6/5/17	Lt. Horn (2)	Nieuport B1539	Albatros D	DOOC	Ecourt-St. Quentin	18.00
6/5/17	Lt. Hunter	Nieuport B1597	Albatros D	DOOC		18.00
	Hunter WIA, FTL, POW; McKissock FTL, POW.					
	(Capt. Bishop 12½ victories confirmed)					
7/5/17	Capt. Bishop (18)	Nieuport B1566	Albatros DIII	DOOC, smoking	N Vitry	09.50
7/5/17	Capt. Bishop (19)	Nieuport B1566	Albatros DIII	DOOC	Brebieres	15.00
	(Pluschow WIA)					
11/5/17	2 Lt. Gunner	Nieuport B1585	Albatros D	DOOC	Douai	14.00
11/5/17	2 Lt. Grandin	Nieuport A6770	Albatros D	DD	Henin	14.00
11/5/17	2 Lt. Jenkins	Nieuport B1566	Albatros D	DOOC	Henin-Brebieres	14.30
11/5/17	2 Lt. Grandin	Nieuport A6770	Albatros D	DD	Brebieres	14.30
11/5/17	2 Lt. Grandin	Nieuport A6770	Albatros D	DD	Brebieres	14.30
11/5/17	Lt. D. R. C. Lloyd	Nieuport B1610	Albatros D	DD	Ecourt-St. Quentin	15.30

DATE	AIRCREW	AIRCRAFT/SERIAL	ENEMY AIRCRAFT	CLAIM	PLACE	TIME
13/5/17	Lt. Fry (6) (+56 Sqn?)	Nieuport B1602	Albatros D	Crashed	Dury	19.25
	(37 victories claimed since 25/3/17, not including KBs)					
19/5/17	Lt. Fry (7)	Nieuport B1602	Albatros DV	FTL	Gouy-en-Artois	10.10
	(796/17 = G39. Ltn. Noth POW)					
	(Lt. Fry: 2½ credited since re-joining 60 Sqn. in April 1917)					
26/5/17	Lts. Fry/D. R. C. Lloyd	Nieuports B1619/B1610	Albatros D	DD	Monchy?	08.30
26/5/17	Capt. Caldwell/2 Lt. Gunner	Nieuports B1618/B1585	Albatros C	DD	Belonne	09.00
26/5/17	Capt. Bishop (20)	Nieuport B1566	Albatros D	DOOC	Izel-les-Epeurchin	10.16
27/5/17	2 Lt. Jenkins	Nieuport B1503	Albatros C	DD	Biache-St. Vaast	06.20
27/5/17	2 Lt. Gunner	Nieuport B1586	Albatros CV?	Destroyed	Vitry	06.30
27/5/17	2 Lt. Phalen	Nieuport B1576	Albatros CV?	Destroyed	Biache	06.40
27/5/17	Capt. Bishop (21)	Nieuport B1566	C	Crashed	Dourges-Monchy	09.40
	(Ulges and von Roebern KIA)					
28/5/17	Maj. Scott (8)	Nieuport B1575	Albatros D	DD	Monchy	07.00
	Scott FTL.					
31/5/17	Capt. Bishop (22)	Nieuport B1566	Albatros DV?	Crashed	Epinoy	07.11
2/6/17	Capt. Bishop (23)	Nieuport B1566	Albatros DIII	Crashed	Estourmel	04.23
2/6/17	Capt. Bishop (24)	Nieuport B1566	Albatros DIII	Crashed	or Esnes	to
2/6/17	Capt. Bishop (25)	Nieuport B1566	Albatros DIII	Crashed	or Awoingt	05.00
5/6/17	Maj. Scott (9)	Nieuport B1575	Albatros DIII	Flamer	Monchy	20.35
	(G43. von Neudorff KIA)					
6/6/17	Lt. Fry & OP	Nieuport B1619	2s	FTL	N Brebieres	09.15
8/6/17	2 Lt. Pope	Nieuport B1652	Albatros CV	DOOC	Vitry	07.45
8/6/17	Capt. Bishop (26)	Nieuport B1566	Albatros DIII	Crashed	N Lille	12.10
	(Bucher KIA?)					
14/6/17	Capt. Caldwell (4)	Nieuport B1654	Albatros D	DOOC	Drocourt	09.55
15/6/17	Lt. D. R. C. Lloyd (3)	Nieuport B1610	Albatros D	DOOC	Vitry	21.00
16/6/17	Capt. Caldwell/Lts. Fry/Collier	Nieuports B1654/B1619/B1605	Albatros DIII	Destroyed	Vitry	20.20
	(Becker WIA)					
16/6/17	Lt. D. R. C. Lloyd (4)	Nieuport B1610	Albatros D	Destroyed	Monchy-Marquion	20.30
	Lloyd and Riessinger KIA in collision					
20/6/17	2 Lts. Penny/Pope	Nieuports B1569/B1679	Albatros D	DOOC	Epeurchin	11.40
21/6/17	2 Lts. Jenkins/Collier/Steele	Nieuports B1629/B1618/B1605	Albatros C	DOOC	Brebieres	07.00
24/6/17	Capt. Bishop (27)	Nieuport B1566	Albatros DIII	Flamer?	Beaumont	11.23?
24/6/17	Capt. Caldwell (6)	Nieuport B1654	Albatros DIII	Crashed	Douai	20.10

DATE	AIRCREW	AIRCRAFT/SERIAL	ENEMY AIRCRAFT	CLAIM	PLACE	TIME
24/6/17	Capt. Caldwell/ Lts. Murray/Adam	Nieuports B1654/B1605/B1569	Albatros DIII	DOOC	Douai	20.10
25/6/17	Capt. Bishop (28)	Nieuports B1566	Albatros DIII	DOOC	Dury	10.25
25/6/17	Lts. Rutherford/Soden/Young	Nieuports B1602/B1598/B1619	Albatros D	DOOC	Dury	10.25
26/6/17	Capt. Bishop (29)	Nieuport B1566	Albatros DIII	Flamer	N Etaing	10.00+
26/6/17	Capt. Bishop (30)	Nieuport B1566	Albatros DIII	DOOC	Annay	10.55
	(Capt. Bishop: 25 victories)					
28/6/17	Capt. Bishop (31)	Nieuport B1566	Albatros DIII	DOOC	Drocourt-La Bassee	11.30?
29/6/17	Capt. Molesworth (6)	Nieuport B1652	Albatros D	Crashed	Douai-Estrees	18.00
	Molesworth FTL					
29/6/17	Lt. Sillars	Nieuport B1698	Albatros D	DOOC, smoking	Douai-Estrees	18.00
29/6/17	2 Lt. G. L. Lloyd	Nieuport B1606	Albatros DIII	Destroyed	Douai-Estrees	18.00
	(von Tutschek FTL at Cantin)					
29/6/17	2 Lt. G. L. Lloyd	Nieuport B1606	Albatros DIII	DOOC	Douai-Estrees	18.15
29/6/17	2 Lt. Jenkins	Nieuport B1629	Albatros D	DOOC	E Lens	18.30
3/7/17	Capt. Caldwell (8)	Nieuport B1654	Albatros D	DOOC	Graincourt	17.50 to
3/7/17	2 Lt. Jenkins/Lt. Adam	Nieuports B1629/B1585	Albatros D	DOOC	Graincourt	
	Adam KIA					
3/7/17	Lt. Soden (2)	Nieuport B1602	Albatros D	DOOC?	Graincourt	18.30
5/7/17	2 Lt. Jenkins & OP	Nieuport B1629	Albatros D	DD	Brebieres	20.00 to
5/7/17	2 Lt. Jenkins & OP	Nieuport B1629	Albatros D	DD	Etaing	
5/7/17	2 Lt. Jenkins & OP	Nieuport B1629	Albatros D	DD	Hendecourt	20.50
	This patrol was operating with F2As; a 4th E/A was also DD.					
7/7/17	2 Lt. G. L. Lloyd (4)	Nieuport B1606	Albatros D	DOOC	Wancourt	11.45
10/7/17	Maj. Scott (10)	Nieuport B1575	Albatros DV	Flamer	Quiery la Motte	20.10
	Scott WIA					
10/7/17	Capt. Bishop (32)	Nieuport B1566	Albatros DIII	DOOC	Vitry-Quiery	20.10
11/7/17	Capt. Molesworth (7)	Nieuport B1652	Albatros D	DOOC	Queant	14.10
12/7/17	Capt. Bishop (33)	Nieuport B1566	Albatros DIII	Crashed	Vitry-Douai	13.40
	(Pastor WIA?)					
12/7/17	Lt. Soden	Nieuport B1598	Albatros D	FTL	Vitry	13.45
13/7/17	2 Lt. Jenkins (10)	Nieuport B1629	Albatros D	DD	Vis-en-Artois	12.00
15/7/17	Capt. Caldwell/ Lts. Jenkins/Sherwood	Nieuports B1654/B1629/B1605	Albatros D	Crashed	Vitry	19.50
	G. A. H. Parkes WIA, FTL, POW					

DATE	AIRCREW	AIRCRAFT/SERIAL	ENEMY AIRCRAFT	CLAIM	PLACE	TIME
15/7/17	Capt. Caldwell/Lts. Jenkins/Sherwood (G56? Pilot POW?)	Nieuports B1654/B1629/B1605	Albatros DV	FTL	Moeuvres	20.15
17/7/17	Capt. Bishop (34)	Nieuport B1566	Albatros DIII	Flamer	Havrincourt	19.43
17/7/17	Capt. Bishop (35)	Nieuport B1566	Albatros DIII	Crashed	Marquion-Queant	19.55
20/7/17	Capt. Bishop (36)	Nieuport B1566	Albatros DIII	DOOC	8 SE Havrincourt	12.05
23/7/17	Capt. Molesworth/Lts. F. Parkes/Penny	Nieuports B1652/B1606/B1608	KB	DD	Recourt	12.30
28/7/17	Capt. Bishop (37)	SE5 A8936	Albatros DIII	Flamer	Phalempin	18.10
29/7/17	Capt. Caldwell (11)	SE5 A8928	Albatros D	DD	W Douai	07.00
29/7/17	Capt. Bishop (38) Gunner KIA	SE5 A8936	Albatros DIII	DOOC	Beaumont	07.10
5/8/17	Capt. Molesworth/Lt. Horn (Lehmann KIA)	SE5s A4851/A8930	Albatros DIII	Flamer	Hendecourt	20.00
5/8/17	Capt. Bishop (39)	SE5 A8936	Albatros DIII	Flamer	Hendecourt	20.00
5/8/17	Capt. Bishop (40)	SE5 A8936	Albatros DIII	DOOC	Monchy	20.20
6/8/17	Capt. Bishop (41)	SE5 A8930	Albatros DIV	Crashed	Brebieres	15.45
9/8/17	Capt. Molesworth (10) (Pilot WIA)	SE5 A8932	Albatros D	Crashed	Cagnicourt	07.00
9/8/17	Lt. Horn (4)	SE5 A8930	Albatros D	Destroyed?	Cagnicourt	07.00
9/8/17	Capt. Bishop (42) (Fl. Abt (A) 288 crew uninjured?)	SE5 A8936	Albatros CV	Crashed	Ecourt-St. Q.	09.00
13/8/17	Capt. Bishop (43)	SE5 A8936	Albatros DIII	Flamer	5 S Douai	19.02
13/8/17	Capt. Bishop (44)	SE5 A8936	Albatros DIII	Flamer	5 S Douai	19.05
15/8/17	Capt. Molesworth/Lts. Pope/Hammond/Beck (suggested that two KBs were DD)	SE5s A8932/A8908/A8914/A8928	KB	DD		06.30?
15/8/17	Capt. Bishop (45)	SE5 A8936	Albatros C	DOOC	Henin-Lietard	20.20
16/8/17	Capt. Bishop (46) (crew KIA?)	SE5 A8936	Aviatik C	Crashed	NE Harnes	19.03
16/8/17	Capt. Bishop (47)	SE5 A8936	Albatros DIII	Crashed	Carvin-Lens	19.06
	(Capt. Bishop: 18 confirmed, 29 DOOC, 2 KB. Capt. Molesworth: 5 confirmed) Ground attack duties for about two weeks.					
26/8/17	Capt. Horn (5) (+ DH 5s)	SE5 A8936	2s	Flamer	Guillemont Farm	07.15
4/9/17	Capt. Horn/Lts. Rutherford/J. Crompton	SE5s A8936/A8934/A8918	Albatros C	FTL	Havrincourt-Brancourt	08.40

DATE	AIRCREW	AIRCRAFT/SERIAL	ENEMY AIRCRAFT	CLAIM	PLACE	TIME
5/9/17	Capt. Horn/ 2 Lts. J. Crompton/Young (Capt. Horn: 4 decisive victories)	SE5s A8936/A8918/A4851	Albatros DV	DOOC	Sailly-en-Ostrevent	19.00+
11/9/17	Lt. Rutherford (Obs. WIA?)	SE5a B520	2s	Damaged	Polygon Wood	10.15
14/9/17	Capt. C-Roberts & OP Hammond FTL, POW	SE5a B4864	Albatros D	DOOC	E Menin	16.45
16/9/17	2 Lt. Pope (4)	SE5 A8933	Albatros D	Crashed	S Houthem	18.30
16/9/17	Capt. C-Roberts/Lt. Whiting Hawtrey WIA, FTL, POW, DOW. (G71. Bauer KIA)	SE5s A8932/A8936?	Albatros DIII	Flamer	S Houthem	18.30
16/9/17	Capt. Hamersley	SE5 A8934	Albatros D	Destroyed	S Houthem	18.30+
17/9/17	Lt. Soden (4)	SE5a B543	Albatros D	DOOC	N Polygon Wood	18.30+
20/9/17	Capt. Law	SE5a B522	Albatros D	DD	E Ypres	11.00+
20/9/17	Lt. Soden (5)	SE5a B510	Albatros D	Crashed	NE Zonnebeke	11.10
20/9/17	2 Lt. J. Crompton (3)	SE5a B543	2s	DOOC	Roulers-Menin	12.45
20/9/17	2 Lt. J. Crompton (4)	SE5a B543	KB	DOOC	Moorslede	13.00+
20/9/17	Lt. Rutherford (4)	SE5a B6	KB	DD?	Roulers	13.00+
20/9/17	Capt. Law	SE5a B535	Albatros D	DOOC	Zonnebeke	16.55
20/9/17	Lts. Jenkins/Macgregor/Elliott Law FTL	SE5a B523/SE5 A8914/ SE5a B4860	Albatros D	DOOC	Zonnebeke	16.55
21/9/17	Lt. Soden (6)	SE5a B523	?	DOOC	Langemark	07.00?
21/9/17	Lt. Young (2)	SE5a B533?	?	Destroyed?	Langemark	14.00
21/9/17	Capt. C-Roberts/Lt. Whiting	SE5 A8932/SE5a B4864	2s	Crashed	Langemark	18.15
21/9/17	Capt. C-Roberts/Lt. Whiting	SE5 A8932/SE5a B4864	Albatros D	Destroyed	Langemark	18.15
21/9/17	Lt. Macgregor (+ SPADs)	SE5a B4860	Albatros D	Crashed	E Ypres	18.15
21/9/17	Lt. Macgregor (3)	SE5a B4860	Albatros D	Crashed	E Ypres	18.45
22/9/17	Capts. C-Roberts/Hamersley Whiting KIA, Macgregor WIA	SE5 A8932/SE5a B539	Albatros D	DOOC	SE Zonnebeke	10.45
22/9/17	Lt. Rutherford (5) (Week ending 24/9/17, 16 E/A crashed by 60 Sqn.)	SE5a B6	2s	Crashed	Ypres-Roulers	18.45
25/9/17	2 Lts. J. Crompton/Young	SE5a B512/B533	Albatros D	Crashed	Goenburg	12.00
25/9/17	2 Lt. Jenkins (14)	SE5a B523	2s	Crashed	1 E Ypres line	15.40
25/9/17	Capt. Caldwell (12) (By 1/10/17: Lt. Soden 2 confirmed)	SE5a B534	2s	DOOC	NE St. Juliaan	16.00
4/10/17	Capt. Caldwell (13)	SE5a B534	Aviatik C	DD	Gheluvelt	11.20

DATE	AIRCREW	AIRCRAFT/SERIAL	ENEMY AIRCRAFT	CLAIM	PLACE	TIME
5/10/17	2 Lt. Fitzgerald / Fitzgerald POW	SE5a B507	?	Crashed?	Menin-Roulers	10.15+
12/10/17	2 Lt. J. Crompton (6)	SE5a B519	Albatros D	Crashed	De Ruite	09.15
12/10/17	Lt. Sherwood (3)	SE5a B523	DFW	DOOC	Moorslede	11.20
21/10/17	Capt. Hamersley (3) (+RE 8 and DH 5)	SE5a B523	Albatros DV	DOOC	Poelcapelle	13.05
21/10/17	Capt. Hamersley (4)	SE5a B523	Albatros DV	DD	Poelcapelle	13.15
21/10/17	Lts. Rutherford/Soden/Young	SE5a B533/B543/B580	2s	Crashed	Houthulst	16.15
28/10/17	Capt. Rutherford (7)	SE5a A8901	Albatros D	DOOC	Westroosbeke	09.30
28/10/17	Capt. Caunter? / Temperley WIA	SE5a B4878	Albatros D	DOOC	Westroosbeke	09.30
30/10/17	Capt. Selous	SE5a B623	2s	DOOC	Moorslede	10.00
1/11/17	Capt. Rutherford/Lt. Soden	SE5a A8934/A8898	Albatros CV?	DOOC	Moorslede	13.45
1/11/17	Capt. Rutherford/Lt. Soden	SE5a A8934/A8898	Albatros C	DOOC	Moorsledge	14.10
1/11/17	Lt. Young	SE5a A8901	Albatros D	DOOC	Houthulst	14.30
5/11/17	Capt. Hamersley (5)	SE5a B626	Albatros D	Crashed	1 N Westroosbeke	12.10
5/11/17	Lt. Soden	SE5a B543	Albatros D	Crashed	Houthulst	12.15
6/11/17	Capt. Rutherford/Lt. Soden	SE5a A8934/B543	2s	Crashed	Zonnebeke	07.30
6/11/17	Lt. W. Duncan / Duncan FTL	SE5a B512	DFW	Crashed	NE Polygon Wood	08.40
8/11/17	Capt. Selous (2) (G88 Steinicke & Brassel KIA)	SE5a B541	Rumpler C	Destroyed	Klein Zillebeke	11.00
8/11/17	2 Lt. Pope (5) (+ two SPADs)	SE5a B533	2s	Crashed	Houthem	11.00
8/11/17	Lt. Pope (6)	SE5a B533	2s	Crashed	Kruiseeck	11.05
8/11/17	Capt. Hamersley (6)	SE5a B4887	Albatros D	Crashed	Westroosbeke	15.40
8/11/17	Capt. Rutherford (11) / McCall FTL	SE5a B608	Albatros D	DOOC	Westroosbeke	15.45
11/11/17	2 Lt. Pope (7)	SE5a B519	Albatros D	Crashed	Gheluwe	15.10
11/11/17	2 Lt. Jenkins (15)	SE5a B608	KB	Flamer	Ypres	15.30?
18/11/17	Capts. C-Roberts/Hamersley / Pope WIA, FTL	SE5a B536/B4887	DFW	Crashed	NE Westroosbeke	11.05
19/11/17	Lts. Jenkins/W. Duncan	SE5a B623/B608	DFW	DOOC	SW Beselare	15.10

DATE	AIRCREW	AIRCRAFT/SERIAL	ENEMY AIRCRAFT	CLAIM	PLACE	TIME
19/11/17	Lts. Jenkins/W. Duncan (+23 Sqn.)	SE5a B623/B608	Albatros C	Crashed	SE Passchendaele	15.45
23/11/17	Capt. C-Roberts (7)	SE5a B536	Albatros DV	Crashed	W Dadizele	10.10
	(4/12/17, Capt. Rutherford: 7 confirmed) (11/12/17, Capt. Chidlaw-Roberts: 5 confirmed, 3 destroyed) Winter training for a few weeks					
18/12/17	Capt. Soden/Lt. Morey	SE5a A8934/B510	Albatros C	DOOC	Gheluvelt	08.15
28/12/17	Soden and Morey FTL (Obs. hit) Capt. Selous (3) (Obs. hit)	SE5a B623	Rumpler C	Crashed	W Roulers	10.45
1/1/18	Capt. Soden/2 Lt. J. Crompton (+23 Sqn.)	SE5a C5332/A8901	DFW	DOOC	W Roulers	10.45
3/1/18	Capt. C-Roberts/ 2 Lt. Cunningham	SE5a C5311/B626	2s	Flamer	Comines-Menin	12.40
9/1/18	Capts. C-Roberts/Soden (+21 Sqn.) (Muller KIA) Poor weather for some weeks	SE5a B626/C5332	Albatros DVa	DD	Moorslede	11.45
24/1/18	Lt. Morey (2) Morey KIA	SE5a B4897	Albatros D	Rammed	Handzame	12.50
25/1/18	Capt. Hamersley (8) (+ 20 Sqn. & DH 4s) (Werner KIA)	SE5a C5321	Albatros DV	Crashed	NE Staden	12.35
28/1/18	2 Lt. Hegarty	SE5a B626	Albatros DV	DOOC	N Kortemark	13.20
28/1/18	Capt. Soden (15) (29/1/18, Capt. Chidlaw-Roberts: 7 destroyed)	SE5a C5332	Albatros D	DOOC	Handzame	13.30
4/2/18	Lts. W. Duncan/Priestley	SE5a C1056/B103	Albatros DVa	Flamer	Ypres	11.20
4/2/18	Lts. H. Crompton/Hegarty (One of these was G131. Langer KIA) (Capt. Soden: 2 confirmed, 3 shared)	SE5a B545/B626	Albatros DVa	Flamer	Zonnebeke	11.25
5/2/18	2 Lt. A. C. Ball	SE5a B533	Albatros DV	DOOC?	Houthulst Wood	10.40
5/2/18	Capt. Soden (16)	SE5a C5332	Albatros DV	DOOC	N Beselare	11.30
5/2/18	Capt. Soden (17)	SE5a C5332	Albatros DV	Crashed	Tenbrielen	11.30+
18/2/18	2 Lt. Hegarty	SE5a C9536	Albatros D	DOOC	Staden	12.30
18/2/18	Capt. Hamersley (9)	SE5a B4487	Fokker DrI	Crashed	N Handzame	12.40 to 13.15
18/2/18	2 Lt. Kent	SE5a B4860	Fokker DrI	Crashed	N Handzame	
18/2/18	2 Lt. Evans/Clark (Etzold KIA)	SE5a B561/C5332	Fokker DrI	Crashed	N Handzame	

DATE	AIRCREW	AIRCRAFT/SERIAL	ENEMY AIRCRAFT	CLAIM	PLACE	TIME
19/2/18	2 Lt. Kent (2) (D4495/17=G 138. Puttkamer POW)	SE5a B4860	Albatros DVa	Flamer	Hollebeke	11.50
	Poor weather for a few weeks					
9/3/18	2 Lt. Griffith	SE5a C5385	Albatros D	DOOC	N Menin	11.10
9/3/18	2 Lt. Evans (2)	SE5a B561	Albatros? Dr	DOOC	N Menin	11.20
9/3/18	Capt. Hamersley (10)	SE5a B4887	Pfalz D	Crashed	Dadizele	11.35
	(Capt. Hamersley: 4 confirmed, 1 shared, 3 DOOC)					
9/3/18	Capt. H. Crompton (2)	SE5a B545	Albatros D	DOOC	Gheluwe	11.40
9/3/18	Lt. W. Duncan (5)	SE5a C9536	Albatros D	DOOC	Gheluwe	11.45
18/3/18	Capt. Hamersley (11)	SE5a C5385	Albatros DVa	Destroyed	Rumbeke	12.50
18/3/18	2 Lt. Griffith (2)	SE5a C1069	Albatros D	DOOC	Roulers	12.50
18/3/18	2 Lt. Cunningham (2)	SE5a C5381	Albatros DV	DOOC	Roulers	12.50
	No combat reports located for period 19–26/3/18, during retreat.					
30/3/18	Capt. Hamersley (12)	SE5a C5385	LVG	Crashed	Mametz Wood	10.55
30/3/18	2 Lt. Proctor	SE5a B4887	Albatros D	DOOC	Albert	11.00
30/3/18	2 Lt. Hegarty (4)	SE5a C5381	Albatros D	Crashed	Treux	11.10
30/3/18	2 Lt. Bartlett	SE5a C5388	Albatros D	DOOC	Hem	11.10
30/3/18	Capt. Copeland	SE5a B190	Albatros C	Crashed	Beire	11.10
30/3/18	Capt. Hamersley	SE5a C5385	Albatros D	DOOC	Fricourt	11.15
30/3/18	Capt. Hamersley (14)	SE5a C5385	Albatros D	Crashed	Hem	11.15
30/3/18	2 Lt. Ortner	SE5a B561	Albatros D	DD	Peronne	11.15
30/3/18	Lts. W. Duncan/Griffith	SE5a C9536/C1069	LVG	Crashed	Becourt	11.50
1/4/18	Lt. W. Duncan (7) (5734/17=G159. Weimar WIA, POW)	SE5a C9536	Albatros DVa	FTL	Gentelles	10.00
1/4/18	Capts. Copeland/Hamersley/ Lts. Priestley/Clark (Obs, hit?)	SE5a B190/B561/D3913/C5332	DFW	DD	Demuin	18.15
2/4/18	Capt. Copeland	SE5a B190	Albatros C	Crashed	Guillaucourt	18.15
2/4/18	2 Lt. Christie	SE5a B8236	Albatros D	Flamer	Rosieres	18.15
	Christie KIA, Campbell FTL (4/4/18, Lt. W. Duncan: 3 confirmed, 1 unconfirmed) Poor weather, ground attack duties, little air opposition for about a month although casualties were sustained in mid-April, 1918.					
6/5/18	Lts. W. Duncan/Griffith	SE5a B567/D3503	Albatros D	Crashed	Guillaucourt	19.15
10/5/18	Lt. Saunders	SE5a C5450	Pfalz D	Destroyed	Bapaume-Peronne	17.35
14/5/18	2 Lt. Hegarty (5)	SE5a B190	Albatros C	Crashed	Moreuil	07.30
15/5/18	Capt. Scholte	SE5a C5385	Rumpler C	Flamer	Lamotte	12.20
15/5/18	Lt. Davies	SE5a D3912	Albatros D	Flamer	Remy	19.45

DATE	AIRCREW	AIRCRAFT/SERIAL	ENEMY AIRCRAFT	CLAIM	PLACE	TIME
15/5/18	Capt. Belgrave	SE5a C1056	Albatros D	Crashed	Arras-Cambrai	19.45
15/5/18	Capt. Belgrave	SE5a C1056	Albatros D	DOOC	Croisilles	19.45+
16/5/18	Capt. Belgrave	SE5a B151	LVG	FTL	NE Arras	08.40
16/5/18	2 Lts. Grifiiths/Hegarty	SE5a D3503/B190	LVG	Crashed	Fampoux	08.45
16/5/18	Capt. Belgrave	SE5a B151	Albatros D	DOOC, smoking	Bapaume	16.15
16/5/18	Lt. Saunders (2)	SE5a C5450	Albatros D	Crashed	Beaulencourt	16.15
	Lt. Proctor KIA					
17/5/18	Capt. Belgrave/	SE5a B151/C5450/B8398	Rumpler	FTL	Contalmaison	05.00
	Lts. Saunders/Lewis					
17/5/18	Lt. W. Duncan (9)	SE5a C9536	Albatros D	Destroyed	Bapaume	11.10
18/5/18	Capt. Belgrave	SE5a B151	DFW	Crashed	Carnoy	11.15
18/5/18	Capt. Belgrave	SE5a B151	Albatros D	DOOC	Carnoy	11.30
19/5/18	Capt. Scholte	SE5a C5385	Hannover CL	Flamer	Arras	10.10
21/5/18	Capt. Belgrave	SE5a D5988	LVG	DOOC	Courcelette	09.30
	(2 Lt. Hegarty: 3 crashed, 2 DOOC. Lt. W. Duncan: 4½ crashed, 1 DOOC)					
23/5/18	Capt. Belgrave/Lt. Saunders	SE5a D5988/B137	Albatros D	Crashed	Fricourt	05.50
28/5/18	Capt. Belgrave	SE5a D5988	LVG	Flamer	Albert	05.10
	(Pilot DOW; Obs. Schroedter? KIA)					
1/6/18	Capt. Belgrave	SE5a D5988	KB	Deflated	Pys	08.00
3/6/18	Capt. W. Duncan	SE5a D5992	LVG CVI?	Crashed	Contalmaison	20.15
4/6/18	Capt. Belgrave/	SE5a D5988/D6183/B8398	KB	DD	Mametz Wood	16.30
	Lts. Saunders/Lewis					
4/6/18	Capt. Belgrave/	SE5a D5988/D6183/B8398	KB	DD	Mametz Wood	16.30
	Lts. Saunders/Lewis					
	(Obs. B/O)					
5/6/18	Lt. Bartlett	SE5a B190	KB	Destroyed	Ervillers	09.20
5/6/18	Lt. McCarthy	SE5a B186	KB	Destroyed	Ervillers	09.25
5/6/18	Capt. W. Duncan	SE5a D5992	KB	Flamer	Irles	09.25
5/6/18	2 Lt. Griffith	SE5a D3503	KB	DD	Cherisy	09.55
	(Obs. seen to B/O of all KBs above)					
5/6/18	Capt. Belgrave	SE5a D5988	Fokker DrI	Flamer	Froyart	19.30
6/6/18	Capt. Duncan	SE5a D5992	LVG CVI?	DD	Hamelincourt	05.40
6/6/18	Capt. Scholte/Lt. Beck	SE5a D6178/D5987	KB	DD	Pys-Susanne	07.25
6/6/18	Lt. Davies	SE5a D6024	KB	DD	Pys-Susanne	07.25
6/6/18	Lt. Clark	SE5a B558	KB	DD	Pys-Susanne	07.25
	(Obs. seen to B/O of all 3 KBs above)					

DATE	AIRCREW	AIRCRAFT/SERIAL	ENEMY AIRCRAFT	CLAIM	PLACE	TIME
9/6/18	Capt. Belgrave/Lt. Saunders	SE5a D5988/B137	Hannover CL	Flamer	Arras	10.45
9/6/18	Capt. Belgrave/Lt. Saunders (Obs. hit?)	SE5a D5988/B137	Hannover CL	DOOC	Arras	10.50
13/6/18	Capt. Belgrave/Lt. Gordon Belgrave KIA	SE5a D5988/E1261	2s	Crashed	4 E Albert	04.45
	(Capt. Belgrave: 6 confirmed in 2 months; Capt. W. Duncan: 6 confirmed)					
	Ground attack and escort duties for two weeks					
30/6/18	Capt. Hegarty (7)	SE5a D5992	Albatros D	Crashed	Rainecourt	05.10
1/7/18	Capt. Hegarty (8)	SE5a D5992	Halberstadt CL.?	Destroyed	Bray	08.40
1/7/18	Lt. Griffith (7) (Obs. B/O)	SE5a D3503	KB	DD	Villers Bretonneux	08.40
1/7/18	Lt. Griffith (8)	SE5a D3503	Albatros DVa	Destroyed	Lamotte	08.45
2/7/18	Lt. Saunders (9)	SE5a E1279	Pfalz DIII	Crashed	Villers Bret.	10.45
2/7/18	Lt. Saunders (10)	SE5a E1279	Pfalz DIII	Crashed	Villers Bret.	10.45+
2/7/18	Lt. Saunders (11) Read WIA	SE5a E1279	Pfalz DIII	Crashed	Villers Bret.	10.45+
	(The latter two E/A collided in this combat over the Bois de Pierret)					
7/7/18	Lt. Griffith (9)	SE5a D5992	DFW	Crashed	Achiet le Grand	11.40
7/7/18	Lt. Whitney	SE5a B186	DFW	Flamer	Achiet le Petit	11.45
	(Lt. Griffith: 3½ confirmed, 2 DOOC, 2 KB; Capt. Hegarty: 5 confirmed, 2 shared, 2 DOOC)					
16/7/18	Lts. Whitney/Bryning/Buckley	SE5a B186/C6359/C8862	KB	DD	Le Sars	16.10
16/7/18	Lts. Whitney/Bryning/Buckley (Obs. B/O of latter KB)	SE5a B186/C6359/C8862	KB	DD	Warlencourt	16.10+
18/7/18	Lt. Whitney (4)	SE5a B186	DFW or LVG	Crashed	Boiry Notre Dame	05.00
22/7/18	Capt. Doyle	SE5a E1288	Pfalz D	DOOC	Avedy Wood	05.40
22/7/18	Lt. Anderson Macvicker KIA	SE5a D6176	Pfalz D	FTL	Avedy Wood	05.40
22/7/18	Lt. Clark & OP	SE5a E1317	KB	DD	S Grevillers	06.15
1/8/18	Capt. Saunders (12)	SE5a E3916	Fokker DVII	DOOC	Bapaume	20.20
3/8/18	Capt. Saunders	SE5a C1937	KB	DD	Martinpuich	17.00
3/8/18	Lt. Beck & OP	SE5a D6945	KB	DD	Sapignies	18.20
4/8/18	Lts. Whitney/Beck	SE5a C8886/D6945	KB	DD	Susanne-Le Sars	06.25
4/8/18	Lts. Whitney/Beck (Obs. B/O)	SE5a C8886/D6945	DFW	DD	Combles/Albert	07.15
8/8/18	Lt. Beck (6)	SE5a D6945	Fokker DVII?	Destroyed	Folies-Rosieres	12.55
8/8/18	Capt. Saunders (14)	SE5a E3916	2s	DOOC	Chaulnes	13.15
8/8/18	Lt. G. Duncan	SE5a D6178	Fokker DVII	Crashed	Peronne	14.00

DATE	AIRCREW	AIRCRAFT/SERIAL	ENEMY AIRCRAFT	CLAIM	PLACE	TIME
8/8/18	Capt. Doyle/Lt. Whitney (crew B/O)	SE5a E1397/C8886	Hannover CL	Crashed	Foucaucourt	16.40
8/8/18	Lts. Whitney/Clark J. G. Hall KIA	SE5a C8886/E3919	DFW	Flamer	Estrees	16.50
8/8/18	Capt. Doyle	SE5a E1397	Hannover CL	Crashed	Estrees	16.55
9/8/18	Capt. Doyle (4)	SE5a E1288	KB	DD	Etaing	08.20
9/8/18	Lt. Whitney	SE5a C8886	KB	DD	Etaing	08.20+
9/8/18	Lts. Clark/Westergaard (Obs. seen to B/O of 1st & 3rd above)	SE5a E3919/E3182	KB	DD	Etaing	08.20+
9/8/18	Capt. Doyle/Lt. Whitney	SE5a E1288/C8886	Hannover CL	Crashed	Croisilles	08.35
9/8/18	2 Lt. Buckley (3)	SE5a C8862	Fokker DVII	Crashed	Marchelpot	15.20
9/8/18	Lt. G. Duncan	SE5a D6178	Fokker DVII	Crashed	Nesles	15.20
9/8/18	Lt. G. Duncan (3)	SE5a D6178	Fokker DVII	DOOC	Chaulnes	15.30
9/8/18	Capt. Saunders	SE5a E3916	Fokker DVII	Crashed	Chaulnes	15.45
9/8/18	Capt. Saunders (16)	SE5a E3916	Fokker DVII	Crashed	Nesles	15.45+
	(Lt. Whitney: 4 confirmed, 1 unconfirmed, 3 and 2 shared crashed, + KBs)					
10/8/18	Lt. G. Duncan (4) Buckley WIA	SE5a D6178	Fokker DVII	Crashed	Foucaucourt	06.45
11/8/18	Capt. Doyle/Lt. G. Duncan	SE5a E1397/D6176	2s	DD	Chaulnes	09.50
11/8/18	Capt. Doyle/Lt. G. Duncan Whitney WIA	SE5a E1397/D6176	2s	DD	Chaulnes	09.50
11/8/18	Lt. Caswell	SE5a C1131	LVG CVI?	Crashed	Ervillers	16.40
12/8/18	Lts. Johnson/Westergaard	SE5a E5991/E3182	2s	FTL?	Croisilles	12.10
14/8/18	Capt. Doyle (8)	SE5a E1397	Albatros D	Crashed	Guemappe	09.45
14/8/18	Lt. Beck (7)	SE5a D6945	Albatros D	Crashed	Guemappe	09.45
17/8/18	Lt. Beck (7)	SE5a D6945	Hannover CL	Crashed	Riencourt	06.15
	Ground attack duties for some days					
22/8/18	Capt. Doyle/Lts. Beck/Oliver (Obs. B/O)	SE5a E1397/D6945/D6887	KB	DD	Haucourt	17.30
22/8/18	Lts. Beck/France	SE5a D6945/D6953	KB	DD	Cagnicourt	17.30+
23/8/18	Capt. Doyle (10)	SE5a E1397	DFW	Crashed	Croisilles	09.55
23/8/18	2 Lt. Sinclair	SE5a E3919	DFW	DOOC	Croisilles	09.55
	(28/8/18, Capt. Doyle: 4½ confirmed, 3 DOOC, + KBs)					
24/8/18	Lts. McCarthy/Millar	SE5a C1937/D361	KB	DD	Vis-en-Artois	15.00
24/8/18	Lts. McCarthy/Millar	SE5a C1937/D361	KB	DD	Vis-en-Artois	15.00
24/8/18	Lts. Beck/Blessley (Obs. hit)	SE5a D6945/D6178	Hannover CL	DD	Croisilles	15.30

DATE	AIRCREW	AIRCRAFT/SERIAL	ENEMY AIRCRAFT	CLAIM	PLACE	TIME
31/8/18	Lts. Beck/Oliver	SE5a D6945/D6887	LVG CVI?	Crashed	Inchy	10.20
31/8/18	Lt. G. Duncan	SE5a D6960	DFW	Crashed	Bapaume	10.20
1/9/18	Capt. Doyle/ Lts. Johnson/Duncan (Obs. fell out)	SE5a E1397/E5991/D6960	KB	DD	Ruyaulcourt	10.10
1/9/18	Capt. Doyle/ Lts. Johnson/Duncan	SE5a E1397/E5991/D6960	KB	DD	Ruyaulcourt	10.10
2/9/18	2 Lt. Sinclair	SE5a E3919	LVG CVI?	Crashed	Bruhemont	10.05
2/9/18	Lt. McCarthy (4) (Obs. hit)	SE5a C1917	LVG CVI?	Damaged	Ecourt-St. Quentin	10.15
2/9/18	Lt. Johnson (4)	SE5a E5991	Albatros D	Crashed	Marquion	19.10
3/9/18	Capt. Doyle (13) Kerr FTL	SE5a D6953	Fokker DVII	Crashed	Inchy	10.10
4/9/18	2 Lt. Sinclair (3)	SE5a E3919	Fokker DVII	Crashed	Rallincourt	06.30
4/9/18	Lt. Johnson (5) Johnson FTL	SE5a E5991	Fokker DVII	Flamer	Epinoy	06.30
4/9/18	Lt. Duncan (5)	SE5a D6960	Fokker DVII	Crashed	Cambrai	06.35
5/9/18	Capt. Doyle	SE5a E1397	Fokker DVII	Flamer	Avesnes	18.10
5/9/18	Capt. Doyle (15) Doyle WIA, FTL, POW	SE5a E1397	Fokker DVII	DOOC	Avesnes	18.10+
5/9/18	Lt. Duncan (6) (Winterfeld KIA?)	SE5a D6960	Fokker DVII	Destroyed	Avesnes	18.20
5/9/18	Lt. Rayner (1) (Pilot B/O)	SE5a D6953	Fokker DVII	Flamer	Avesnes	18.20
5/9/18	Lt. Rayner (2) Blessley WIA	SE5a D6953	Fokker DVII	DOOC	Avesnes	18.25
5/9/18	Lt. Duncan (7)	SE5a D6960	Fokker DVII	DOOC	Avesnes	18.25
(7/9/18, Lt. G. Duncan: 5 confirmed, 2 DOOC; Lt. Beck: 4 crashed, KB DD)						
Poor weather and ground attack duties for a few days.						
28/9/18	Capt. Beck (5)	SE5a F5455	LVG CVI?	Crashed	Cambrai	08.25
Poor weather and ground attack duties for a few days						
3/10/18	Capt. Beck	SE5a F5455	Fokker DVII	DOOC	Esnes	08.15
3/10/18	Lt. L. H. Smith	SE5a E5694	Fokker DVII	DOOC	Esnes	08.15+
3/10/18	2 Lt. Mason	SE5a C1937	Fokker DVII	Flamer	Malincourt	14.45
Poor weather and ground attack duties for a few days						
9/10/18	Capt. Beck (6)	SE5a F5455	LVG CVI?	Flamer	Bohain	11.40
Poor flying weather intervened again for about a week						

DATE	AIRCREW	AIRCRAFT/SERIAL	ENEMY AIRCRAFT	CLAIM	PLACE	TIME
22/10/18	Capt. Beck	SE5a F5455	Halberstadt CLIV?	FTL	Ovillers	16.15
23/10/18	Capt. Rayner (3)	SE5a D6953	Fokker DVII	DOOC	Selesches	14.30
23/10/18	Lt. McCarthy (5)	SE5a E6007	Fokker DVII	DOOC	Selesches	14.30
23/10/18	Capt. Beck	SE5a F5455	LVG CVI?	DD	Selesches	15.10
	2 Lt. Densham FTL					
25/10/18	Capt. Rayner	SE5a D6953	Fokker DVII	Flamer	Berlaimont	09.50
25/10/18	Capt. Rayner (5)	SE5a D6953	Fokker DVII	DOOC	Berlaimont	09.50
25/10/18	2 Lt. Mason (2)	SE5 C1937	Fokker DVII	DOOC	Berlaimont	09.50
25/10/18	2 Lt. Burbidge	SE5a F5507	Fokker DVII	DOOC	Berlaimont	09.50
25/10/18	Lt. L. H. Smith	SE5a E1276	Fokker DVII	Crashed	Berlaimont	09.50
	Smith FTL, POW (Pilot B/O of this latter E/A)					
26/10/18	Capt. Beck/Lt. Orpen	SE5a F5455/E6029	LVG CVI?	Crashed	Le Quesnoy	13.25
	(Obs. B/O)					
28/10/18	Capt. Beck	SE5a F5455	LVG CVI?	DD	Valenciennes	12.50
	Stockwell FTL, POW					
29/10/18	2 Lt. Mason (3)	SE5a C1937	Fokker DVII	Crashed	Landrecies	14.40
29/10/18	2 Lt. Burbidge (2)	SE5a F5507	Fokker DVII	DOOC	Mormal	14.40
29/10/18	Capt. Beck (8)	SE5a D6953	Fokker DVII	DOOC	Mormal	14.50
30/10/18	Capt. McEntegart	SE5a D6136	LVG CVI?	Destroyed	Mormal	09.30
	(+ SE5as from another Sqn.)					
1/11/18	Lt. McCarthy (6)	SE5a E6007	Fokker DVII	DOOC	Bavai	15.35
1/11/18	Lt. McCarthy/Capt. Beck/	SE5a E6007/D6134/D380	Fokker DVII	Crashed	Mormal Wood	16.00
	2 Lt. Newth					
2/11/18	Capt. Beck	SE5a D6134	LVG CVI?	FTL?	NE Le Quesnoy	08.30
	(Capt. Beck: 9 confirmed; 2 Lt. Mason; 3 confirmed; Capt. Rayner: 4 confirmed?)					

APPENDIX IV

A BRIEF HISTORY OF SIXTY SQUADRON
1920 TO 1990

After its highly successful years in France, Sixty Squadron was reduced to Cadre on 5 May, 1919, and returned to the UK, and was disbanded on 22 January, 1920.

However, this famous Squadron was retained for peacetime service, and on 1 April, 1920, No. 97 Sqn., in India, was re-numbered 60, which thereafter took part in most of the numerous campaigns on the North West Frontier as a bomber squadron until 1939. The bombers used by the Squadron in this period were successively DH 10, DH 9A, and Wapiti biplanes.

In March, 1939, the Squadron was withdrawn from duty on the Frontier in order to re-equip with the first Blenheim bombers to arrive in India. With the outbreak of war in Europe, coastal patrol duties were undertaken from airfields by the major ports around India. The Japanese threat resulted in the Squadron moving to Rangoon in February, 1941, thus becoming the first squadron to be based in Burma. By December, most of the Squadron was on detachment in Malaya for an Armament Practice Camp, and thus took part in raids against the Japanese invasion force. By Christmas, 1941, Squadron personnel were withdrawn from Singapore, back to Rangoon. However, replacement aircraft and crews were inadequate to stem the Japanese advance into Burma, so personnel were evacuated to India in February, 1942, to re-equip with Blenheim Mk. IV bombers. Until May, 1943, the Squadron bombed Japanese targets in Burma.

Thereafter, the Squadron was re-equipped with Hurricane fighter-bombers, and resumed operations. In March, 1944, the Squadron was transferred to Assam and played a significant part in the defence of Imphal, and the subsequent advance to Rangoon. When the Japanese surrendered, the Squadron was converting to Thunderbolts, and subsequently served in Indonesia until November, 1946.

Continuing in the fighter-bomber role, the Squadron then played a major part in the Malayan Emergency, using Spitfires, Vampires and Venoms in succession, based mainly in Singapore. Thereafter, a change in role occurred in 1959, when Meteor and then Javelin night/all-weather fighters were introduced for the defence of Malaysia. This involved further action against Indonesian insurgents in the Confrontation against Malaysia, operating from airfields in Singapore, Malaya, and Malaysian Borneo.

Subsequently, British military forces in the East were reduced, and Sixty Squadron was disbanded in 1968. Within a year, the Communications Squadron in RAF Germany was numbered Sixty, and continues in that role to this day, flying Andover and Pembroke aircraft.

D. W. Warne
1990

INDEX